SIDE BY SIDE
ACTIVITY WORKBOOK

2A

Steven J. Molinsky
Bill Bliss

Illustrated by
Richard E. Hill

Contributing Authors

Elizabeth Handley
Katharine Kolowich
with
Mary Ann Perry

Editorial Development

Tina B. Carver

PRENTICE HALL REGENTS, Englewood Cliffs, NJ 07632

Prentice-Hall International, Inc., *London*
Prentice-Hall of Australia Pty. Limited, *Sydney*
Editora Prentice-Hall do Brasil, Ltda., *Rio de Janeiro*
Prentice-Hall Canada Inc., *Toronto*
Prentice-Hall of India Private Limited, *New Delhi*
Prentice-Hall of Japan, Inc., *Tokyo*
Prentice-Hall of Southeast Asia Pte. Ltd., *Singapore*
Whitehall Books Limited, *Wellington, New Zealand*

Contents

A. WHAT'S HAPPENING?

What	bake	drink	go	plant
Where	buy	eat	move	swim

1

1. __*What's*__ Mrs. Green __*drinking?*__

   __*She's drinking*__ coffee.

2. _____ Jennifer _____?

   _____ to a concert.

3. _____ Mr. Williams _____?

   _____ flowers.

4. _____ you and your friend

   _____?

   _____ ice cream.

5. _____ Mr. and Mrs. Hardy _____?

   _____ to Centerville.

6. _____ you _____?

   _____ a chocolate

   cake.

7. _____ Mr. and Mrs. Jones _____?

   _____ presents for their

   children.

8. _____ Roger _____?

   _____ at the beach.

1

B. ON THE PHONE

1.

Hi. What _____are_____ you doing?

_____ dinner.

I'm sorry. I always call at the wrong time. _____ Tom busy?

Yes, _____. _____ a shower. Can we call you later?

Sure. I'll be home all evening.

2.

Hi. _____ you and Harry doing today?

Not very much. Right now _____ reading.

Why don't we all go to a concert together?

That's a great idea.

3.

Hello, Janet. _____ the children O.K.?

Yes. _____ fine.

What _____ they doing?

Mary _____ for her English examination, and the boys _____ TV.

Tell them I'll be home soon.

2

4.

Hello, Jim. This is Uncle Ted. _____ your father there?

No, he isn't. _____ late at the office.

May I speak to your mother?

I'm afraid she can't come to the phone right now. _____ very busy.

Really? _____ doing?

_____ the sink. It's broken.

That's too bad. I guess I'll call back later.

5.

Hello, ... Can I speak to . . . . ?

I'm sorry . . . .

. . . .

Well, can I speak to . . . . ?

I'm afraid . . . .

. . . .

I guess I'll call back later.

C. **YOU DECIDE:** *WHY IS TODAY DIFFERENT?*

1. (smoke) I never _____*smoke*_____ cigarettes, but _____*I'm smoking*_____ today

   because . . . .

2. (wear) George never _____ a tie, but _____ a tie today

   because . . . .

3. (work) We never _____ late at the office, but _____ late today

   because . . . .

4. (argue) Michael never _____ with his brother, but _____ with him

   today because . . . .

5. (send) Mario never _____ his girlfriend flowers, but _____ her

   flowers today because . . . .

6. (study) Elizabeth never _____, but _____ today

   because . . . .

7. (take) Mr. and Mrs. Smith never _____ the subway, but _____

   the subway today because . . . .

8. (watch) Our teacher never _____ TV, but _____ TV today

   because . . . .

9. (write) My older brother never _____ to our family, but _____ to

   us today because . . . .

10. (get up) Janet never _____ early, but _____ early today

    because . . . .

11. (drink) Mr. and Mrs. Jones never _____ champagne, but _____

    champagne today because . . . .

12. (go) Susan never _____ to restaurants, but _____ to a

    restaurant today because . . . .

13. (smile) Mr. Sharp never _____, but _____ today

    because . . . .

D. WHAT ARE THEY SAYING?

1. Lois plays the piano beautifully.

   Does her daughter _play_ the piano well?

2. My brother lives in Chicago.

   _____ your sister _____ there, too?

3. My son gets up at 6:00 every morning.

   _____ you _____ early, too?

4. Our daughter goes to the movies every week.

   _____ you and your wife _____ to the movies very often?

5. Robert likes classical music.

   _____ he _____ popular music, too?

6. Tommy and Nancy watch TV all afternoon.

   _____ they _____ TV in the evening?

7. Hilda bakes delicious bread.

   _____ cookies, too?

8. Alice and I usually walk to work.

   _____ to work in the winter?

9. Boris speaks French and Russian.

   _____ English, too?

10. William and Richard work at night.

    _____ during the day?

11. Norman has two grandsons.

    _____ any granddaughters?

12. Frieda and Julie always complain about school.

    _____ about their teacher?

13. I drink three cups of coffee every morning.

    _____ a lot of coffee during the day?

14. Margaret always worries about her daughter.

    _____ about her son?

E. WHAT'S THE WORD?

1. I _don't_ like to go dancing with Peter because he _____ a good dancer.

   I know. Everybody says _____ very clumsy.

2. My sister _____ a very good singer.

   I don't agree with you. I think she _____ beautifully. _____ very talented.

3. My mother _____ like to ride to work with me because she thinks _____ a terrible driver. She's wrong! I _____ very carefully.

4. Shirley _____ going swimming with us today because she _____ like to swim when it's cold.

   That's too bad. I really like to go swimming with her. She's an excellent _____.

5. My husband and I _____ very good skaters, but we like to _____ anyway.

   _____ you like to ski?

   No, we _____. _____ afraid we might get hurt.

6. I'm really jealous of my brothers.

   Why?

   Because _____ very good athletes, and I'm not.

   Don't be ridiculous! Your brothers _____ tennis very well, but you're a good tennis _____, too.

   _____ you really think so?

   Of course I _____.

6

F. LISTEN

Listen to each question, and then complete the answer.

1. Yes, _____*he does.*_____
2. Yes, _____*she is.*_____
3. Yes, _____.
4. Yes, _____.
5. No, _____.

6. No, _____.
7. Yes, _____.
8. No, _____.
9. Yes, _____.
10. Yes, _____.

11. No, _____.
12. Yes, _____.
13. No, _____.
14. No, _____.
15. Yes, _____.

G. WHAT'S THE QUESTION?

1. He's writing to <u>his sister</u>.   *Who's he writing to?*

2. They're visiting <u>their friends</u>. _____

3. She's complaining about <u>her examination</u>. _____

4. I'm calling <u>my boss</u>. _____

5. She's thinking about <u>her new job</u>. _____

6. He's shouting at <u>his landlord</u>. _____

7. We're waiting for <u>the bus</u>. _____

8. They're talking about <u>their vacation</u>. _____

9. He's arguing with <u>his son</u>. _____

10.  I'm writing about <u>my favorite movie</u>. _____?

H. WHAT ARE THEY SAYING?

1. A. Why is Tom visiting ___his___ aunt.

   B. ___He___ wants to tell ___her___ about this afternoon's football game.

2. A. Why is Mrs. Brown calling _____ neighbors?

   B. _____ wants to tell _____ about _____ vacation.

3. A. Why are David and Frank complaining about _____ teacher?

   B. _____ gives _____ too much homework.

4. A. Why are you calling _____ friend Peter so late?

   B. _____ want to talk to _____ about tomorrow's examination.

5. A. Why are you and _____ friends studying so late?

   B. If _____ don't finish this book tonight, _____ teacher will be angry at _____ .

6. A. Why is Mrs. Watson writing to _____ son?

   B. _____ wants to wish _____ "Happy Birthday."

7. A. What are your parents giving _____ for your birthday, Johnny?

   B. I'm not sure, but _____ might give _____ an electric train.

8. A. Why is Mr. Young shouting at _____ daughter?

   B. _____ forgot to ask _____ before she took the car this afternoon.

9. I want to tell _____ and Dad about the party last night.

   Why are you up so early? Go back to sleep! You can

   tell _____ about _____ later.

8

I. WHAT'S THE WORD?

1. Carmen always complains [at / **about**] the weather in Chicago.

2. Call [to / at] the plumber right away!

3. Why is Jim arguing [at / to / with] his little sister?

4. Judy writes [at / to / from] her boyfriend twice a week.

5. Mrs. Morgan doesn't like to shout [at / to / ___] her children.

6. Mrs. Lopez visits [at / to / ___] her sister whenever she goes [at / to / ___] Miami.

7. I'm helping [at / to / ___] my daughter [to / with / ___] her homework.

8. Mr. Crabapple is frustrated because he has to wait [for / ___ / at] the bus.

9. Why does Charlie always talk [at / ___ / about] his problems?

10. My parents are watching [to / ___ / at] their favorite TV program.

11. Who's feeding [to / at / ___] the dog today?

A. A TERRIBLE NIGHTMARE

It (be) ___*was*___ midnight, and I (be) _____ at a party at a friend's house
when the babysitter (call) _____. "Come home right away!", she said.

I didn't stop to ask any questions. I (get) _____ into my car and (drive)
_____ home as quickly as possible. But when I (reach) _____
River Street, the most dangerous street in town, I (get) _____ a flat tire.

It (be) _____ very dark and quiet, and I (be) _____ terribly afraid.
I (start) _____ to walk down the street, when I (see) _____ an
enormous dog. He (look) _____ very angry, and he (bark)
_____ when he (see) _____ me. What (can) _____ I do?
I (have) _____ to think quickly. Fortunately, I (have) _____ some food from
the party with me. I (take) _____ some cookies from my pocket, and I (give)
_____ them to the dog. He (stop) _____ barking right away, and he
(eat) _____ the cookies. While he was eating, I (walk) _____ away.

A half hour later, I finally (arrive) _____ home. I (look)
_____ in my pocket for the key, but it wasn't there. I guess I (lose)
_____ it when I was feeding the dog. I (decide) _____ to get into the
house through the living room window.

A few minutes later, I (be) _____ in the living room. I didn't see or hear
anything strange, so I (go) _____ upstairs. Then somebody (shout)

_____, "Help!" I (be) _____ so nervous that I (trip) _____
over a chair and (fall) _____ down. Then. . . . .

. . . .

. . . .

. . . .

. . . .

. . . .

I'm glad it was only a dream.

B.   LISTEN

Listen and put a circle around the correct words.

1. yesterday **every day** (circled)	6. last Friday / every Friday	11. yesterday / every day
2. **yesterday evening** (circled) / every evening	7. yesterday morning / every morning	12. yesterday / every day
3. yesterday / every day	8. last night / every night	13. yesterday afternoon / every afternoon
4. yesterday evening / every evening	9. last week / every week	14. yesterday evening / every evening
5. last week / every week	10. yesterday morning / every morning	15. yesterday morning / every morning

11

Listen and fill in the missing words. Then read the passage aloud.

My parents _____needed_____ a lot of help when they moved to their new house. I _____
heavy furniture for them, and I _____ all the rooms. When I _____ one day, my
mother said she _____ a garden. I _____ until spring, and then I _____
one. I _____ flowers and vegetables in the yard.

Yesterday my brother _____ to move. I'm not complaining. I really like to help.
But I think I'll be busy for a while!

D. WHAT'S THE QUESTION?

1. _____*Did you go*_____ to the movies? No, I didn't. I went to a concert.

2. _____ anything for me? No, I didn't. I bought something for your mother.

3. _____ her glasses? No, she didn't. She forgot her pocketbook.

4. _____ German? No, he didn't. He taught French.

5. _____ by plane? No, they didn't. They came by train.

6. _____ a stomachache? No, she didn't. She had a cold.

7. _____ Martin? No, I didn't. I saw his sister.

8. _____ his English homework? No, he didn't. He did his math homework.

9. _____ your record player? No, they didn't. They stole our money.

10. _____ a red umbrella? No, I didn't. I lost a blue one.

E. SOMETHING DIFFERENT

1. David usually has yogurt for lunch.

    He ___*didn't*___ ___*have*___ yogurt for lunch yesterday.

    He ___*had*___ a salad.

2. Barbara usually sits by herself in English class.

    She _____ _____ by herself yesterday.

    She _____ with her friends.

3. We usually buy ice cream for dessert.

    We _____ _____ ice cream yesterday.

    We _____ strawberries.

4. Our music teacher usually sings very well.

    She _____ _____ very well yesterday.

    She _____ badly.

5. Sally and Carl usually go to work by car.

    They _____ _____ to work by car yesterday.

    They _____ to work by taxi.

6. I usually drink a lot of coffee.

    I _____ _____ any coffee yesterday.

    I _____ a lot of tea.

7. My grandmother usually gives me a tie for my birthday.

    She _____ _____ me a tie this year.

    She _____ me a shirt.

8. Eleanor usually takes a ballet lesson on Tuesday.

    She _____ _____ a ballet lesson last Tuesday.

    She _____ a piano lesson.

9. We usually get home at 5:00.

    We _____ _____ home at 5:00 yesterday.

    We _____ home very late.

10. Irene usually drives carefully.

    She _____ _____ carefully yesterday.

    She _____ much too fast.

11. Ted usually rides his motorcycle.

    He _____ _____ his motorcycle yesterday.

    He _____ his bicycle.

12. Mr. Warren usually teaches science.

    He _____ _____ science this year.

    He _____ math.

F. WHAT ARE THEY SAYING?

1. _____*Did you clean*_____ the basement?

   No, _____. I _____ too tired. But I cleaned my room.

2. _____ to Albert yesterday?

   No, I _____. I talked to his wife.

   Albert _____ there when I called.

3. _____ you see Paul at the party last Saturday?

   No, we _____. But we _____ his wife.

4. _____ you write to Mr. Jones yesterday?

   No, I _____. I _____ too busy.

   But I _____ to Mr. Henderson.

5. _____ Peggy _____ her motorcycle to work this morning?

   No, she _____. She rode her bicycle, and she _____ late.

14

6. _____ you read Chapter One last night?

Yes, _____. _____ it twice because it _____ so interesting.

7. _____ Mrs. Nelson teach English last year?

Yes, _____. And she _____ history, too.

_____ you in her class?

No, we _____.

8. _____ the children eat a big lunch?

Yes, _____. They _____ so hungry that they _____ three sandwiches.

9. _____ buy anything at the store?

Yes, I _____. _____ some food for tonight.

_____ any oranges?

No, I didn't. There _____ any fresh ones.

10. What's the matter? _____ hurt your back?

No, I _____. _____ my arm.

I guess I _____ very careful.

15

G. **HOW DID IT HAPPEN?**

1. How did Alice hurt herself?   (play soccer)

   She hurt herself while she was playing soccer.

2. How did Martin burn himself?   (iron his clothes)

   _____

3. How did Helen cut herself?   (slice onions)

   _____

4. How did Jennifer meet her husband?   (fix a flat tire)

   _____

5. How did Marvin break his arm?   (skate)

   _____

6. How did you lose your wallet?   (ride my bicycle)

   _____

7. How did Jeff meet his wife?   (swim at the beach)

   _____

8. How did Bob get a black eye?   (fight with his brother)

   _____

9. How did your children burn themselves?   (make breakfast)

   _____

10. How did Martha trip and fall?   (dance)

   _____

11. How did you . . . . ?

. . . .

That's too bad.

H. A VACATION

Use these pictures as a guide to write about a vacation.

....

....

....

....

....

....

....

....

....

....

....

....

....

....

I. WHAT'S THE QUESTION?

how	how many	what kind of	where	why
how long	what	when	who	

1. _____*Who did you visit*_____?   I visited my cousin.

2. _____?   We talked about my job.

3. _____?   She went to the beach.

4. _____?   She met her friend.

5. _____?   They spoke Russian.

6. _____?   They swam in the ocean.

7. _____?   He had dinner at 8:00.

8. _____?   I baked an apple pie.

9. _____?   She cried because her dog ran away.

10. _____?   I stayed for a week.

11. _____?   I came home by train.

12. _____?   He ate three hamburgers.

13. _____?   He left the restaurant at 9:00.

14. _____   They covered their eyes because they

_____?   were scared.

15. _____?   She wrote a letter to her mother.

16. _____?   They meditated all morning.

17. _____?   We took a lot of photographs.

18. _____?   We sent a postcard to our teacher.

19. _____?   He fell asleep during the lecture.

20. _____?   I lost my wallet while I was skating.

J.   SOUND IT OUT

Listen to each word and then say it.

this:

1. v<u>i</u>sit
2. W<u>i</u>lliam
3. mus<u>i</u>c
4. f<u>i</u>sh
5. b<u>u</u>sy
6. <u>i</u>sn't

these:

1. w<u>ee</u>kend
2. b<u>ea</u>ch
3. happ<u>y</u>
4. rec<u>ei</u>ve
5. St<u>e</u>ve
6. <u>ea</u>sy

Listen and put a circle around the word that has the same sound.

1. f<u>i</u>nish: f<u>i</u>ne   ⟨w<u>i</u>nter⟩   p<u>i</u>zza
2. s<u>i</u>t: <u>i</u>nteresting   <u>i</u>ron   <u>ea</u>t
3. m<u>ea</u>t: br<u>ea</u>d   br<u>ea</u>k   mov<u>ie</u>s
4. t<u>ee</u>th: h<u>i</u>story   s<u>ee</u>   gr<u>ea</u>t
5. l<u>i</u>sten: p<u>ie</u>ce   n<u>i</u>ght   d<u>i</u>d
6. st<u>ea</u>l: dent<u>i</u>st   an<u>y</u>   w<u>ea</u>ther
7. l<u>i</u>ft: L<u>i</u>nda   l<u>i</u>fe   f<u>ee</u>t
8. r<u>i</u>p: sm<u>i</u>le   th<u>ie</u>f   th<u>i</u>s

Now make a sentence using all the words you circled. Read the sentence aloud.

9. _____ _____ _____ _____ _____ _____

    _____

10. d<u>i</u>sh: tr<u>i</u>cks   t<u>ea</u>ch   br<u>ie</u>fcase
11. gr<u>ee</u>n: healthy   w<u>ea</u>r   thr<u>ee</u>
12. m<u>i</u>x: ch<u>i</u>ld   mag<u>i</u>c   pl<u>ea</u>se
13. n<u>ee</u>d: Ir<u>e</u>ne   m<u>e</u>n   r<u>ea</u>dy
14. l<u>i</u>ttle: exerc<u>i</u>se   <u>i</u>s   spaghett<u>i</u>
15. b<u>i</u>g: pract<u>i</u>cing   w<u>i</u>ne   adv<u>i</u>ce
16. sw<u>i</u>m: pol<u>i</u>ce   r<u>i</u>pe   d<u>i</u>fficult

Now make a sentence using all the words you circled. Read the sentence aloud.

17. _____ _____ _____ _____ _____ _____ _____

A. WHAT ARE THEY SAYING?

3

1. Did we give our granddaughter a watch for her birthday this year?

   _____No, we didn't._____ We ___gave___ her a gold bracelet. ___We're going___ ___to give___ her a watch next year.

2. Did your sister go out on a date with Robert last night?

   _____. She _____ out with Tom. _____ _____ out with Robert tomorrow night.

3. Did you write an interesting story for homework today?

   _____. I _____ a very boring one. _____ _____ a more interesting story next time.

4. Did Tom and Sheila drive to Los Angeles last weekend?

   _____. They _____ to San Francisco. _____ _____ to Los Angeles next weekend.

5. Did you wear your new shoes to school yesterday?

   _____. I _____ my boots. _____ _____ my new shoes tomorrow.

6. Did you and your friends read Shakespeare in class last semester?

   _____. We _____ Hemingway. _____ _____ Shakespeare next semester.

20

7. Did Billy send a birthday present to Uncle Jim last week?

_____. He _____ one to Uncle Barney. _____ _____ a birthday present to Uncle Jim next week.

8. Did you leave work early last night?

_____. I _____ work very late. _____ _____ work early tonight.

9. Did you do your English homework last night?

_____. I _____ my Spanish homework. _____ my English homework tonight.

10. Did you and Ronald eat at home last night?

_____. We _____ at Stanley's International Restaurant. _____ at home tonight.

11. Did you see the new science fiction movie at the Rix Theater last night?

_____. I _____ a western at the Regency. _____ _____ the new science fiction movie at the Rix Theater tonight.

12. Did Mom and Dad speak to the landlord about our broken window?

_____. They _____ to him about the cockroaches in the kitchen. _____ to him about our broken window the next time they see him.

21

B. BAD CONNECTIONS

1. I'm so nervous. Tomorrow my doctor is going to ########

   I'm sorry. I can't hear you. I think we have a bad connection. What's _your doctor going to do?_

2. I'm really excited about my vacation. We're going to go #######

   What did you say? I can't hear you. Where _____ _____?

3. My son is really disappointed. His best friend is going to move because ######

   I'm sorry. We have a terrible connection. Why _____ _____?

4. My parents are going to give me a ######### for my twenty-first birthday.

   Excuse me. I can't hear you. _____ _____?

5. My daughter is really looking forward to this Saturday night. She's going to go out with ##########

   We have a bad connection. _____ _____?

6. Please come to our wedding. We're going to get married next #############

   I'm sorry. I can't hear you. _____ _____?

7. I won't be home tomorrow. I'm going to visit ####### in the hospital.

   We have a very bad connection. _____ _____?

8.

Peggy and John are going to name their new baby ##########

What did you say? I can't hear you very well. _____

_____

_____?

9.

Mr. Smith. I'm going to fire you because #### ##########

Excuse me, sir. I think we have a bad connection.

_____

_____?

10.

And after we steal the money, you and I are going to go #########

What??!! I can't hear you.

_____

_____?

C. I'M AFRAID

Michael is a pessimist. He always thinks the worst will happen.

1. I'm afraid I _____*won't have*_____ a good time at Robert's party this weekend.

2. I'm afraid my daughter _____*will*_____

_____*catch*_____ a cold in the park today.

All his friends are optimists. They always tell Michael he shouldn't worry.

1. Yes, _____*you will.*_____

We're sure _____*you'll*_____ have a wonderful time!

2. No, _____*she won't.*_____

_____*She*_____ _____*won't*_____ catch a cold today. She's wearing a warm sweater.

3. I'm afraid my car _____

_____ on cold mornings this winter.

4. I'm afraid my children _____

_____ my birthday this year.

5. I'm afraid my landlord _____

_____ my broken sink.

6. I'm afraid I _____ happy in my new job.

7. I'm afraid my son _____
a car accident. It's raining very hard.

8. I'm afraid I _____
weight on my new diet.

9. I'm afraid my wife _____

_____ my new haircut.'

10. I'm afraid my neighbors _____

_____ angry because I'm having a big
party tonight.

3. Yes, _____. We're

sure _____ start every morning.

4. No, _____. We're

sure _____ forget
your birthday!

5. Yes, _____. We're sure

_____ fix it as soon as he can.

6. Of course _____.

_____ be very happy in your new
job.

7. No, _____. We're sure

_____ have an accident.
He's a careful driver.

8. Yes, _____. Of course

_____ lose weight.
Don't worry about it!

9. We're sure _____.

_____ like your haircut a lot.
You look terrific!

10. No, _____.

_____ be angry.
Why don't you invite them, too?

D. EVERYBODY'S BUSY

1. Will Jane be busy tonight?

   Yes, _____she will._____

   _____She'll be studying_____ English
   until ten o'clock.

2. Will you be busy this evening?

   Yes, _____. _____

   _____ until 10 or
   11 o'clock.

3. Will Mr. and Mrs. Morgan be busy
   today?

   Yes, _____.

   _____
   until about 4:30.

4. Will Peggy be busy tomorrow morning?

   Yes, _____. _____

   _____ all morning.

5. Will Frank be busy today?

   Yes, _____. _____

   _____ all day.

6. Will Alan be busy after dinner?

   Yes, _____. _____

   _____ for an hour
   or two.

7. Will your sister be busy this morning?

   Yes, _____. _____

   _____ for several
   hours.

8. Will you and your husband be busy tonight?

   Yes, _____. _____

   _____ at Franklin's
   International Discotheque until midnight.

25

E. A TOUR OF MY CITY

Pretend you're taking people on a tour of your city or town. Fill in the blanks with real places you know.

Good morning, everybody. This is . . . . speaking. I'm so glad you'll be coming with me today on a tour of . . . . We'll be leaving in just a few minutes.

First, I'll be taking you to see my favorite places in the city: . . . . ,

. . . . , and . . . .

Then we'll be going to . . . . for lunch. In my opinion, this is the best restaurant in town. After that, I'll be taking you to see the other interesting tourist

sights: . . . . , ... ,

and . . . . This evening we'll be going to . . . .

. . . . I'm sure you'll all have a wonderful time.

F.   DID YOU HEAR?

mine
his
hers
ours
yours
theirs

ANNE: Did you hear what happened last night?

BETTY: No, I didn't. What happened?

ANNE: The police found a blue car in the park down the street. All the windows were broken and the radio was missing. I hope that blue car isn't ___yours.___

BETTY: I don't think so. I'm sure my husband drove _____ to work this morning. Could it be Mr. Anderson's car? _____ is blue.

ANNE: No, I don't think so. _____ is at the repair shop.

BETTY: How about Mrs. Taylor? Maybe it's _____. I think she has a blue car.

ANNE: No. I don't think so. _____ isn't blue. I think it's green.

BETTY: How about Mr. and Mrs. Lane? Don't they have an old blue car? Maybe it's _____.

ANNE: No, it can't be _____. They moved away last month.

BETTY: How about YOU, Anne? Are you SURE it isn't _____?

ANNE: I'm positive! I know it isn't _____. My car is in front of the house. Wait a minute. I'll look out the window right now.

BETTY: Is it still there? Do you see it?

ANNE: Oh no! It isn't there. I'm afraid the car in the park might be _____.

BETTY: Maybe you should call the police.

27

G. **WHAT DOES IT MEAN?**

Put a circle around the correct answer.

1. He's composing a symphony.
   a. He's writing a symphony.
   b. He's listening to a symphony.
   c. He's going to a concert.

2. Michael has a black eye.
   a. He painted his eye.
   b. He hurt his eye.
   c. He's wearing dark glasses.

3. Mr. and Mrs. McCarthy are meditating.
   a. They're eating very slowly.
   b. They're talking.
   c. They're sitting quietly with their eyes closed.

4. I'm going to fill out my income tax form.
   a. I'm going to return my income tax form.
   b. I'm going to answer the questions on my income tax form.
   c. I'm going to read my income tax form.

5. Can I borrow your hammer?
   a. I need your hammer for a little while.
   b. I want to give you my hammer.
   c. I want to buy your hammer.

6. She wasn't prepared for her exam.
   a. She didn't take her exam.
   b. She didn't study for her exam.
   c. She was ready for her exam.

7. I'm going to lend my car to Bill today.
   a. I'm going to give my car to Bill.
   b. I'm going to drive Bill's car.
   c. Bill is going to give me his car.

8. Mr. Warren is looking forward to his retirement.
   a. He's happy about his new job.
   b. He wants to buy new tires for his car.
   c. Soon he won't have to go to work every day.

9. My sister is arguing with her boyfriend.
    a. They're having a good time.
    b. They don't agree about something.
    c. They agree about something.

10. I'm going to repair my brother's bicycle.
    a. I'm going to paint it again.
    b. I'm going to fix it.
    c. I'm going to ride it.

11. Could you possibly do me a favor?
    a. I want to help you.
    b. I want to give you something.
    c. I need your help.

12. Edward is complaining to his boss.
    a. He's talking about his boss and he's very upset.
    b. He's talking to his boss and he's very happy.
    c. He's talking to his boss and he's very upset.

13. I'm going to call my husband right away.
    a. I'm going to call him immediately.
    b. I'm going to call him in a few hours.
    c. I'm going to call him when I have the time.

14. Sarah is looking for a magazine.
    a. She's looking for a store.
    b. She's looking for something to read.
    c. She's looking for the second floor.

15. My parents are going to relax this weekend.
    a. They're going to retire this weekend.
    b. They're going to exercise this weekend.
    c. They're going to rest this weekend.

H. LISTEN: *LOOKING FORWARD*

Listen and answer the questions after each story.

What's Henry Looking Forward To?

1. _____
2. _____
3. _____

What's Bobby Looking Forward To?

1. _____
2. _____
3. _____
4. _____

What's Julie Looking Forward To?

1. _____
2. _____
3. _____
4. _____
5. _____

CHECK-UP TEST: Chapters 1-3

A. Fill in the blanks.

Ex. Mary ___*is*___ a good skier, and her children

___*ski*___ well, too.

1. A. George and Peter _____ wonderful
        swimmers.

    B. I agree with you. They _____ very
        well.

2. A. Helen _____ carelessly.

    B. I know. _____ a terrible driver.

3. A. I don't skate very well.

    B. I don't agree with you. I think

        _____ an excellent

        _____.

4. We _____ good tennis

    _____, but we like to _____
    tennis anyway.

B. Fill in the blanks.

1. A. Did you write to Mr. Jones yesterday?

   B. No, I _____. I _____ too

      busy. But I _____ to Mr. Lee.

2. A. Did you buy any milk when you

      _____ at the store?

   B. No, I _____. I forgot. But I

      _____ some orange juice.

3. A. _____ Mrs. Armstrong teach French
      last year?

   B. No, she _____. She

      _____ Spanish because the

      Spanish teacher _____ sick all
      semester.

4. A. _____ you speak to Jennifer
      yesterday?

   B. No, I _____. I _____

      to her husband. Jennifer _____
      there when I called.

5. A. _____ Louise eat her dinner last
      night?

   B. Yes, she _____. She _____ so

      hungry that she _____ three
      hamburgers.

6. A. Did your children _____ up on time
      this morning?

   B. No, they _____. They

      _____ so tired that they got up at
      noon.

C. Write the question.

Ex. We're arguing with our neighbors.

   Who are you arguing with?

1. I'm writing about my favorite book.

   _____

2. They're going to call the landlord.

   _____

3. She swam in the ocean.

   _____

4. He'll be ready in a few minutes.

   _____

5. They came by boat.

   _____

6. She's going to take five photographs.

   _____

7. We'll be staying in London until Tuesday.

   _____

D. Answer the questions.

Ex. What did Tom do yesterday morning?

(ride his bicycle) _____ *He rode his bicycle.* _____

1. What's Nancy doing today?

(visit her neighbors) _____

2. What does Jim do every afternoon?

(watch TV) _____

3. What are you and your friends doing today?

(have a party) _____

4. What did Roger and Jack do yesterday afternoon?

(go bowling) _____

5. What was Dan doing when his wife came home?

(bake bread) _____

6. What are you going to do tomorrow?

(clean my apartment) _____

7. What will you and your husband be doing this evening?

(play cards) _____

8. How will your daughter get to school tomorrow if it snows?

(take the bus) _____

E. Listen to each question and then complete the answer.

Ex. Yes, _____ *she does.* _____

1. Yes, _____.   5. No, _____.

2. Yes, _____.   6. Yes, _____.

3. No, _____.   7. No, _____.

4. Yes, _____.   8. No, _____.

A. NOT TODAY

1. Donald isn't going to go to the beach today.

   ___*He's*___ already ___*gone*___ to the beach this week.

   ___*He went*___ to the beach yesterday.

2. I'm not going to write to my granddaughter today.

   _____ already _____ to her this week.

   _____ to her on Monday.

3. Shirley isn't going to eat any pizza tonight.

   _____ already _____ pizza this week.

   _____ pizza on Friday.

4. We aren't going to do our laundry today.

   _____ already _____ our laundry this week.

   _____ our laundry yesterday.

5. Ted isn't going to wear his black suit today.

   _____ already _____ his black suit this week.

   _____ it on Saturday.

6. Alan and Irene aren't going to take a violin lesson today.

   _____ already _____ a violin lesson this week.

   _____ a violin lesson on Tuesday.

7. Frank isn't going to give his girlfriend flowers tonight.

_____ already _____ her flowers this week.

_____ her flowers on Sunday.

8. We aren't going to spend a lot of money at the store today.

_____ already _____ a lot of money at the store this week.

_____ a lot of money yesterday.

9. I'm not going to buy any tomatoes today.

_____ already _____ a lot of tomatoes this week.

_____ a dozen tomatoes on Thursday.

10. Mary isn't going to swim today.

_____ already _____ this week.

_____ on Saturday.

11. Sam isn't going to cook French food today.

_____ already _____ French food this week.

_____ French food on Wednesday.

12. Henry and Walter aren't going to go bowling today.

_____ already _____ bowling this week.

_____ bowling on Tuesday.

B. WHAT ARE THEY SAYING?

1.
A. Peggy, you've got to take a bath.

B. But, Mother, ____I've____ already _____ a bath this week.

A. Really? When?

B. Don't you remember? _____ a bath on Sunday.

2.
A. Would you like to see a movie today?

B. I don't think so. _____ already _____ a movie this week.

A. Really? When?

B. _____ a movie on Monday.

3.
A. Are you going to go on vacation soon?

B. No. _____ already _____ on vacation.

A. Oh, that's right. I forgot. _____ on vacation last January.

4.
A. I hope Timmy gets a haircut soon.

B. Don't worry, Mother. _____ already _____ one.

A. I'm glad to hear that. When?

B. _____ a haircut yesterday.

A. That's wonderful.

C. IN A LONG TIME

clean	fix	read	write
dance	go	see	
do	have	study	
eat	practice	take	

1. Rover looks hungry. He _hasn't eaten_ anything in a long time.

2. I'm very sorry, but I _____ _____ in a long time.

3. I really think Johnny should go to school today. He _____ to school in a long time.

4. What's the matter, Theodore? You aren't playing very well.

I know. I _____ in a long time.

5. Marylou's room is very dirty.

I know. She _____ it in a long time.

6. I'm really excited. I'm going to see my grandmother today. I _____ her in a long time.

7. All my clothes are dirty. I don't have anything to wear.

I know. I _____ the laundry in a long time.

8. The landlord says he's going to fix our washing machine today.

I don't believe it. He _____ _____ anything in our apartment in a long time.

9. When are you going to take me to a baseball game? You _____ _____ me to one in a long time.

10. I think Charlie watches too much TV. He _____ a book in a long time.

11. Who was the sixteenth president of the United States?

I can't remember. I _____ _____ American history in a long time.

12. I hope Carol and Arthur are O.K.

They _____ to us in a long time.

13. We _____ a quiet evening together in a long time.

37

D. WHAT ARE THEY SAYING?

1. _Have_ you _gone_ to the post office yet?

Yes, _I have._ I went there this morning.

2. _____ Kathy _____ to you yet?

Yes, _____. She wrote to me last week.

3. _____ you and Alan _____ the play at the Grant Theater yet?

Yes, _____. We saw it last night.

4. _____ Robert _____ his new tuxedo yet?

Yes, _____. He wore it last Sunday.

5. _____ your parents _____ you to the new candy store yet?

Yes, _____. They took me there yesterday.

6. _____ you and your wife _____ any plans for the summer yet?

Yes, _____. We made them last week.

7. _____ Susan _____ your parents yet?

Yes, _____. She met them last weekend.

8. _____ you _____ your homework yet?

Yes, _____. I did it this afternoon.

9. _____ Sharon and Charles _____ home yet?

Yes, _____. They got home a few minutes ago.

10. _____ you _____ Henry his birthday present yet?

Yes, _____. I gave it to him this morning.

11. _____ Norman _____ his new motorcycle yet?

Yes, _____. He rode it this afternoon.

38

E. A LOT OF THINGS TO DO

William is going to have a party tonight,
and he has a lot of things to do.

☑ go shopping	1. _____ *He's already gone shopping.* _____
☐ clean my apartment	2. _____ *He hasn't cleaned his apartment yet.* _____
☐ get a haircut	3. _____
☑ bake bread	4. _____
☐ make dessert	5. _____
☑ fix the record player	6. _____

Tom and Lucy are going to go on
vacation tomorrow, and they have a lot
of things to do.

☐ do our laundry	7. _____
☑ pay our electric bill	8. _____
☐ pack our suitcases	9. _____
☑ return our library books	10. _____
☑ buy a new tennis racket	11. _____
☐ say good-bye to our neighbors	12. _____

Jane has a lot of work to do at the office today.

☑ write to Mrs. Peters	13. _____
☐ call Miss Watson	14. _____
☑ take Mr. Warren to lunch	15. _____
☐ meet with Mr. Grant	16. _____
☑ send income tax forms to	17. _____
the new employees	_____
☐ fire Mr. Smith	18. _____

You have a lot of things to do today.
What have you already done?
What haven't you done yet?

1. ....
2. ....
3. ....
4. ....
5. ....
6. ....

F. IS OR HAS?

1. He's already eaten dinner.

   _____ is

   ✔ has

2. He's eating dinner.

   ✔ is

   _____ has

3. She's washing her car.

   _____ is

   _____ has

4. She's given us a lot of homework this week.

   _____ is

   _____ has

5. He's having a terrible time.

   _____ is

   _____ has

6. She's going to leave.

   _____ is

   _____ has

7. He's bought a lot of clothes recently.

   _____ is

   _____ has

8. It's raining.

   _____ is

   _____ has

9. She's hungry.

   _____ is

   _____ has

10. He's got to study.

    _____ is

    _____ has

11. Where's the nearest restaurant?

    _____ is

    _____ has

12. She's written to her family.

    _____ is

    _____ has

13. He's taking a lot of photographs.

    _____ is

    _____ has

14. He's taken a few photographs.

    _____ is

    _____ has

15. He's spent all his money.

    _____ is

    _____ has

16. There's a laundromat across the street.

    _____ is

    _____ has

17. She's gone shopping.

    _____ is

    _____ has

18. It's very cold.

    _____ is

    _____ has

19. He's embarrassed.

    _____ is

    _____ has

20. This is the best science fiction book she's ever read.

    _____ is

    _____ has

41

G. **WHAT ARE THEY SAYING?**

1. A. I'm upset. I ____wrote____ a letter to Mary last month, and she _____ _____ back yet.

    B. Don't worry. I'm sure _____ write to you soon.

2. A. _____ you seen Arthur's new motorcycle yet?

    B. No, _____. When _____ he get it?

    A. He _____ it yesterday, and _____ already ridden it everywhere.

    He _____ it to my house yesterday afternoon.

3. A. Have you _____ any good movies recently?

    B. No, I _____. I _____ a movie a week ago, but it was terrible.

    A. Really? What movie did _____?

    B. "The Magnificent Monkey." It's one of the worst movies I've ever _____.

4. A. _____ you spoken to Donald recently?

    B. Yes, _____. I _____ to him yesterday.

    A. What _____ he say?

    B. He's worried because he _____ done his English homework in a long time, and his

    teacher is _____ give an English test tomorrow.

5. A. What _____ you get for your birthday yesterday?

   B. My parents _____ me twenty-five dollars.

   A. That's great! What _____?

   B. Going to buy? I've already _____ all my birthday money.

   A. Really? What _____ buy?

   B. I _____ four Beatles' records. Would you like to hear them?

6. A. Are you ready to leave?

   B. No, _____. I haven't _____ a bath yet.

   A. I don't believe it! You _____ up an hour ago. You're really slow today. _____ you eaten breakfast yet?

   B. Of course, _____. I _____ a little while ago, and I've already _____ the dishes.

   A. Well, hurry up! It's 8:30, and I don't want to be late.

H. LISTEN

Listen to each word and then say it.

{j!}

1. jacket
2. January
3. jelly
4. Jimmy
5. jogging
6. journalist
7. just
8. pajamas

{y!}

1. yard
2. year
3. yellow
4. yesterday
5. yet
6. yogurt
7. young
8. New York

I.   _ULIA'S BROKEN T_PEWRITER

Julia's typewriter is broken. The j's and the y's don't always work. Fill in the missing j's and y's, and then read Julia's letters aloud.

1.

J udy,
    Did I leave my blue and **y** ellow
__acket at __our house __esterday
after the __azz concert? I __ust
can't find it anywhere.
                              __ulia

2.

__eff,
    __ack and I are out __ogging,
but we'll be back in __ust a few
minutes. Make __ourself comfortable.
__ou can wait for us in the __ard.
If __ou're thirsty, take some
__uice from the refrigerator.
                              __ulia

3.

Dear __ennifer,
    We're sorry __ou and __oe can't
visit us this __une. Do __ou think
__ou can come in __uly? We really
en__oyed __our visit last __ear.

                              __ulia

4.

Dear __ane,
    Thank __ou very much for the
beautiful pa__amas you sent
__immy. He received them
__esterday. __immy is too
__oung to write to __ou himself,
but he says, "Thank __ou." I'm
sure he'll en__oy wearing his
new pa__amas on cold __anuary
nights.
                              Love,
                              __ulia

5.

__ack,
    We need a __ar of __elly, a
large can of orange __uice, and
some __ogurt. Would __ou please
buy them when __ou go to the
store today?
                              __ulia

6.

Dear __anet,
    We got a letter from George
__ackson __ust last week. He's
really en__oying college this
__ear. His favorite sub__ects
are German and __apanese. He's
looking for a __ob in New __ork
as a __ournalist, but he hasn't
found one __et.
                              __ulia

A. HOW LONG?

| for | since |

5

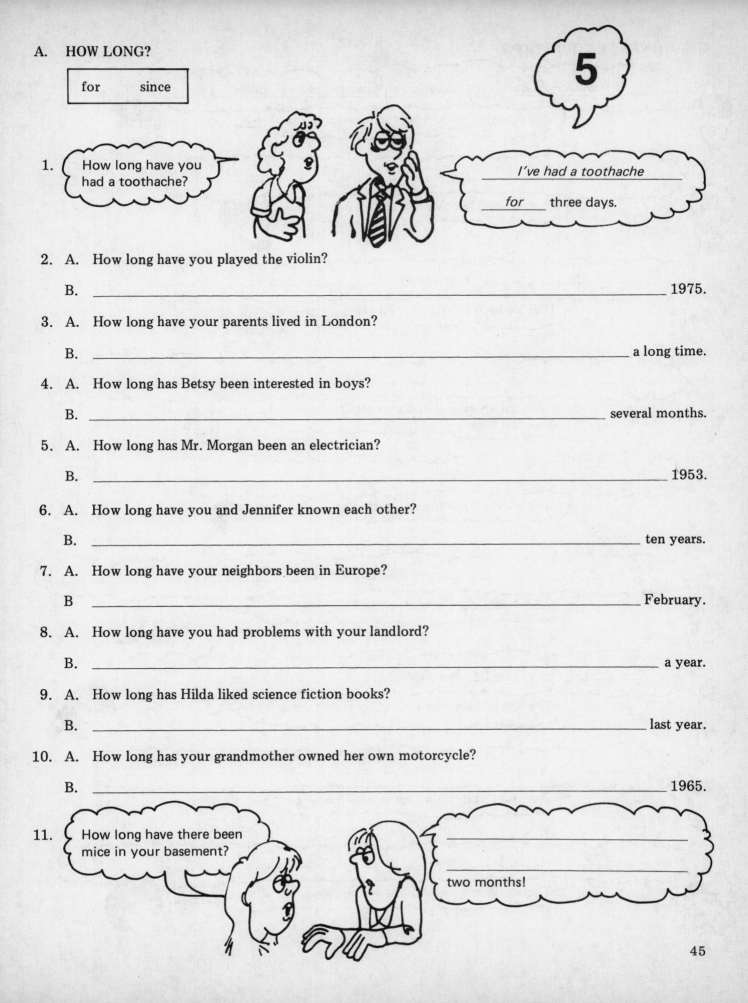

1. How long have you had a toothache?

   I've had a toothache _____ *for* three days.

2. A. How long have you played the violin?

   B. _____ 1975.

3. A. How long have your parents lived in London?

   B. _____ a long time.

4. A. How long has Betsy been interested in boys?

   B. _____ several months.

5. A. How long has Mr. Morgan been an electrician?

   B. _____ 1953.

6. A. How long have you and Jennifer known each other?

   B. _____ ten years.

7. A. How long have your neighbors been in Europe?

   B _____ February.

8. A. How long have you had problems with your landlord?

   B. _____ a year.

9. A. How long has Hilda liked science fiction books?

   B. _____ last year.

10. A. How long has your grandmother owned her own motorcycle?

    B. _____ 1965.

11. How long have there been mice in your basement?

    _____

    _____

    two months!

45

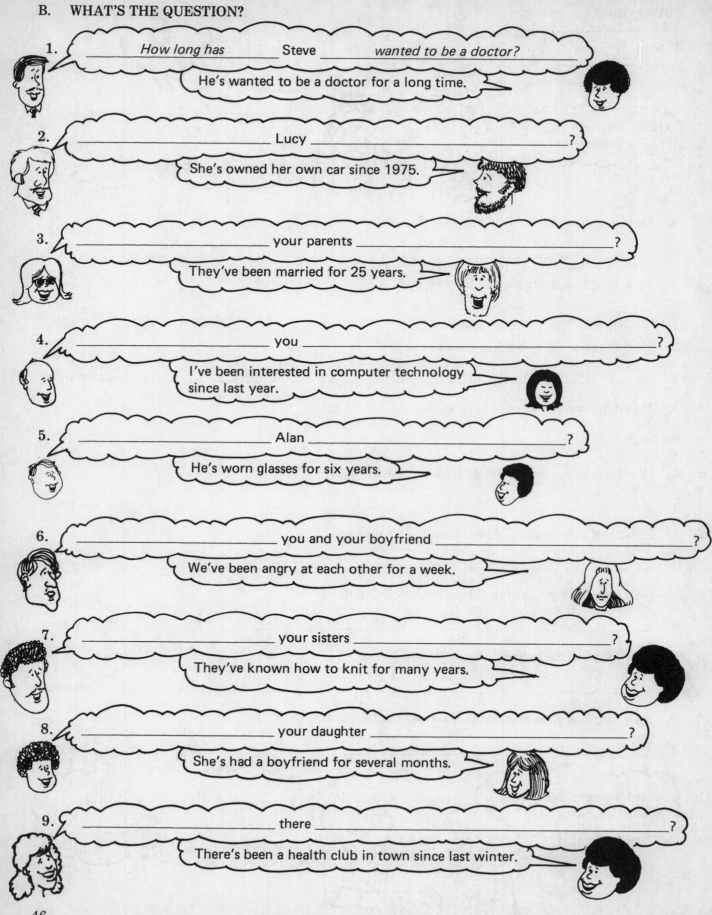

1. _____ *How long has* _____ Steve _____ *wanted to be a doctor?*

He's wanted to be a doctor for a long time.

2. _____ Lucy _____?

She's owned her own car since 1975.

3. _____ your parents _____?

They've been married for 25 years.

4. _____ you _____?

I've been interested in computer technology since last year.

5. _____ Alan _____?

He's worn glasses for six years.

6. _____ you and your boyfriend _____?

We've been angry at each other for a week.

7. _____ your sisters _____?

They've known how to knit for many years.

8. _____ your daughter _____?

She's had a boyfriend for several months.

9. _____ there _____?

There's been a health club in town since last winter.

C. SINCE WHEN?

1. _____I'm_____ very tired today.

   _____I've been_____ tired since I got up this morning.

2. Nancy _____ very well.

   _____ very well since she was six years old.

3. _____ lost.

   _____ lost since we arrived here four hours ago.

4. _____ cloudy.

   _____ cloudy since last week.

5. _____ nervous.

   _____ nervous since I got married a few hours ago.

6. Fred _____ very hard.

   _____ hard since he came here two months ago.

7. My kitchen sink _____ broken.

   _____ broken since yesterday morning.

8.

My neighbors _____ every night.

_____ every night since they moved here last month.

9.

My sister _____ the violin very well.

_____ very well since she was four years old.

10.

My children and I _____ very cold.

_____ cold since the radiator broke two hours ago.

11.

I _____ a backache.

_____ a backache since I played basketball with my son this morning.

12.

My boyfriend _____ bored.

_____ bored since this movie started three hours ago.

13.

My feet _____.

_____ since I hiked ten miles last weekend.

D. SCRAMBLED SENTENCES

Unscramble the sentences.

1. last   had   Helen   a   night   headache   has   since

   _____

2. he   little   the   since   played   a   boy   he's   violin   was

   _____

3. history   I've   in   I   Greek   interested   since   Athens   been   visited

   _____

4. since   Paul   been   they   and   college   Sara   engaged   have   finished

   _____

5. piano   how   since   we've   young   to   the   known   play   very   were   we

   _____

6. professional   you   wanted   a   to   musician   ten   you've   years   since   old
   be   were

   _____

E. WRITE ABOUT YOURSELF

1. I'm interested in . . . .

   I've been interested in. . . . . .since . . . .

2. I like . . . .

   I've . . . . .since . . . .

3. I want to. . . . .

   I've. . . . . .since . . . .

4. I know how to . . . .

   I've. . . . . .since . . . .

49

F. THEN AND NOW

go	like	teach
have	live	visit

1. Mr. and Mrs. Grant ___go___ to the

   symphony every week. _____

   _____ to the symphony every week since
   they moved to the city. Before that,

   _____ never _____ to the
   symphony. They stayed home and listened
   to records.

2. Before she moved to Mexico, Professor Wilson

   _____ French. Now _____

   _____ Spanish. _____

   _____ Spanish at a Mexican
   university for the past three years.

3. I _____ in an apartment since
   1978. Before I got my own apartment,

   _____ with my
   parents.

4. Henry doesn't like rock and roll music

   anymore. _____ it when he

   was in high school, but now _____

   _____ jazz. _____
   jazz for many years.

5. Your Aunt Gertrude _____ already

   _____ us five times this year!

   Last year, she _____ us only twice.

   How many times will she _____ us
   next year?!

6. Nelson _____ a lot of gray hair now.

   _____ a lot of gray hair since
   he started to teach English five years ago.

   Before that, _____ black hair.
   We all think he worries too much!

G.   LOOKING BACK

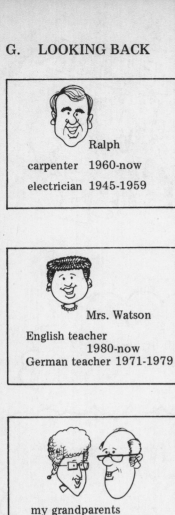

Ralph

carpenter   1960-now

electrician   1945-1959

Mrs. Watson

English teacher
        1980-now
German teacher 1971-1979

my grandparents

Democrats   1973-now

Republicans   1930-1973

Maria
(work)

bank   1975-now

post office   1964-1975

Bob and Betsy
(live)

Madrid   1977-now

Toronto   1975-1977

1. How long _____*has Ralph been*_____ a carpenter?

    _____*He's been a carpenter*_____ since _____*1960.*_____

2. How long _____*was he*_____ an electrician?

    _____ for _____.

3. How long _____ an English teacher?

    _____ for _____.

4. How long _____ a German teacher?

    _____ for _____.

5. How long _____ Republicans?

    _____ for _____.

6. How long _____ Democrats?

    _____ since _____.

7. How long _____ at the bank?

    _____ since _____.

8. How long _____ at the post office?

    _____ for _____.

9. How long _____ in Toronto?

    _____ for _____.

10. How long _____ in Madrid?

    _____ since _____.

H. HIGH SCHOOL REUNION

1. Do you still go dancing every weekend?

No. . . . .

. . . .(for/since). . . . .

. . . .

2. Do you still lift weights every morning?

No. . . . .

. . . .(for/since). . . . .

. . . .

3. Are you still a Republican?

No. . . . .

. . . .(for/since). . . . .

. . . .

4. How long have you been interested in

. . . .?

. . . .

. . . .(for/since). . . . .

. . . .

5.

Is your sister still a professional basketball player?

No. . . . .
. . . .(for/since) . . . .

6.

Do your brothers still call you "Shorty"?

No. . . . .
. . . .(for/since) . . . .

7.

How long have you . . . .
. . . . ?
. . . .
. . . .(for/since) . . . .

8.

Do you still . . . .
. . . . ?

No. . . . .
. . . .(for/since) . . . .

53

I. LISTEN: *THE BAKER FAMILY*

Listen to the story and fill in the information. Then use the information to answer the questions below.

1. Mr. Baker

    a. math teacher: for _____

    b. before that: _____

2. Mrs. Baker

    a. professional violinist: since _____

    b. symphonies: _____

3. Jeff

    a. sports car driver: for _____

    b. computers: since _____

4. Nancy

    a. winter sports: since _____

    b. ski: for _____

5. Charlie

    a. count to a hundred: since _____

    b. play the violin: for _____

Listen and answer each question in a complete sentence.

1. _____

2. _____

3. _____

4. _____

5. _____

6. _____

7. _____

8. _____

9. _____

10. _____

A. HOW LONG?

1. How long has Bill been sleeping?

   He's been sleeping since 10:00 last night.

2. How long have Bill and Mary been watching TV?

   several hours.

3. How long has Betsy been making her own clothes?

   she got married.

4. How long have we been jogging?

   ten minutes.

5. How long has Professor Jones been talking?

   two hours.

6. How long have Louise and Jeffrey been dancing?

   the party began.

7. How long have you been teaching?

   1950.

8. How long have I been lying here?

   a week.

9. How long has Marylou been studying?

_____

early this morning.

10. How long have you and your wife been skating?

_____

three hours.

11. How long have Mr. and Mrs. Baker been meditating?

_____

a half hour.

12. How long has Billy been crying?

_____

his sister ate his ice cream.

B. WHAT ARE THEY DOING?

1. (read)   Tom _____*is reading.*_____

   _____*He's been reading*_____ since noon.

2. (work)   Mrs. Thompson _____.

   _____ since early this morning.

3. (bake)   My sister and I _____ cookies.

   _____ cookies for several hours.

4. (ride)   Steve _____ his bicycle.

   _____ his bicycle since 3:00.

5. (fight)   You and your brother _____.

   _____ all morning.

6. (write)   Shirley _____ her English composition.

   _____ her English composition for an hour.

7. (take care of)   Fred _____ his little brother.

   _____ his little brother since 6:00.

8. (complain)   My parents _____.

   _____ since I broke the living room window this morning.

56

C. SOUND IT OUT

Listen to each word and then say it.

<u>this</u>:

1. w<u>i</u>nter
2. dent<u>i</u>st
3. ch<u>i</u>cken
4. l<u>i</u>ft
5. b<u>ui</u>lding
6. <u>i</u>tself

<u>these</u>:

1. agr<u>ee</u>
2. sp<u>ea</u>k
3. br<u>ie</u>fcase
4. arm<u>y</u>
5. f<u>e</u>ver
6. <u>ea</u>ten

Listen and put a circle around the word that has the same sound.

1. s<u>i</u>ck:	pol<u>i</u>ce	t<u>i</u>red	(h<u>i</u>s)
2. t<u>ee</u>nager:	h<u>ea</u>dache	t<u>ea</u>cher	sw<u>ea</u>ter
3. s<u>ee</u>n:	P<u>e</u>ter	b<u>ee</u>n	fl<u>y</u>
4. h<u>i</u>mself:	w<u>i</u>ll	dec<u>i</u>de	tax<u>i</u>
5. asl<u>ee</u>p:	m<u>e</u>t	<u>e</u>vening	clin<u>i</u>c
6. f<u>i</u>shing:	sc<u>i</u>ence	wr<u>i</u>ting	h<u>i</u>story
7. l<u>ea</u>ve:	s<u>ee</u>ing	h<u>ea</u>vy	discoth<u>e</u>que
8. m<u>i</u>lk:	h<u>i</u>re	s<u>i</u>dewalk	th<u>i</u>s
9. ch<u>ea</u>p:	tr<u>i</u>p	b<u>e</u>	<u>i</u>nterested

Now make a sentence using all the words you circled. Read the sentence aloud.

10. _____ _____ _____ _____ _____ _____ _____ _____

11. g<u>i</u>ven:	<u>ea</u>sy	<u>i</u>sn't	dr<u>i</u>ving
12. betw<u>ee</u>n:	d<u>i</u>nner	beg<u>i</u>n	he'll
13. <u>i</u>nterview:	b<u>i</u>cycle	th<u>i</u>s	<u>i</u>ron
14. tenn<u>i</u>s:	b<u>u</u>sy	th<u>e</u>se	p<u>ie</u>ce
15. angr<u>y</u>:	t<u>y</u>pe	v<u>i</u>olin	w<u>ee</u>kend
16. p<u>eo</u>ple:	L<u>i</u>nda	G<u>i</u>nger	St<u>e</u>ve
17. tr<u>i</u>ck:	Gr<u>ee</u>k	<u>i</u>f	ch<u>i</u>ld
18. w<u>i</u>sh:	v<u>i</u>sit	sl<u>i</u>ce	athl<u>e</u>te
19. y<u>ea</u>r:	w<u>ea</u>r	m<u>e</u>	h<u>ea</u>rt

Now make a sentence using all the words you circled. Read the sentence aloud.

20. _____ _____ _____ _____ _____ _____ _____ _____

D. WHAT ARE THEY SAYING?

cry	rain	wait
live	smoke	wear
play	study	work

1.

Mrs. Harris, please come home soon. The baby is crying, and I don't know what to do.

Has he been crying for a long time?

Yes, he _____. _____ all evening.

2.

My doctor says I should stop smoking, but I don't think I'll be able to.

_____ for a long time?

Yes, I _____. _____ for more than twenty years.

3.

I'm sorry I'm late. _____ for a long time?

No, I _____. I just got here a few minutes ago.

4.

Have you met our new secretary yet?

No, I _____. How long _____

_____ here?

_____ here for three days.

5.

What a terrible day! _____

_____ for a long time?

Yes, it _____. _____ since 5:00 this morning.

6.

_____ in Centerville for a long time?

No, _____. I just moved here last week.

58

7.

Your son and daughter speak English very

well. _____ it
for a long time?

Yes, they _____. _____
English for five years.

8.

Your shirt is very dirty. _____
it all week?

No, _____. I just put it on this
morning.

9.

This is the tenth chess game you've won

today. _____ for
a long time?

No, I _____. _____
for only a few months.

Really? I don't believe it.

E. **YOU DECIDE:** *WHAT HAVE THEY BEEN DOING?*

1. I have a sore throat.   No wonder you have a sore throat!   *You've been singing (or)*
    . . . .
    You've been talking   all day.
    . . . .

2. Sally and Andy can't finish   No wonder they can't finish their dinner! . . . .
    their dinner.
    . . . . all day.

3. My feet hurt.   No wonder your feet hurt! . . . .
    . . . . all day.

4. Carl has a headache.   No wonder he has a headache! . . . .
    . . . . all day.

5. David doesn't have any money.   No wonder he doesn't have any money! . . . .
    . . . . all week.

6. George and his wife are   No wonder they're depressed! . . . .
    depressed.
    . . . . all day.

7. Julie looks very healthy.   No wonder she looks healthy! . . . .
    . . . . all summer.

F. WHAT'S HAPPENING?

eat	meet	read	swim
give	paint	smoke	talk
listen	play	study	type

1. My son and daughter are very tired. _____*They've been studying*_____ since they got home from school. *They've* already _____*studied*_____ French, English, and history. They won't be able to go to sleep until very late tonight. _____ mathematics yet.

2. Sally is exhausted. _____ her apartment since 10:00 this morning. _____ already _____ the bathroom, the living room, and the kitchen. And she isn't finished. _____ _____ her bedroom yet!

3. Mr. Arnold is enjoying himself. _____ since noon. _____ already _____ six short stories.

4. My husband and I are very full. _____ for the last two hours. _____ already _____ a lot of soup, salad, chicken, and potatoes. And our dinner isn't finished. _____ _____ our dessert yet!

5. Steve is very nervous. _____ cigarettes all day. _____ already _____ three packs.

6. Frieda is getting tired. _____ for an hour. _____ already _____ across the pool twenty times.

7. Mr. and Mrs. Anderson are enjoying themselves. _____

_____ cards since 5:00 this

evening. _____ already _____ ten games, and they

_____ lost one yet.

8. I'm having a wonderful time. _____

to music all morning. _____ already _____ to all my

favorite records.

9. Sarah is really tired. _____ since she

got to work. _____ already _____ 15 letters.

10. Mr. and Mrs. Grant love to talk. _____

all evening. _____ already _____ about their

family, their friends, and their vacation. (Fortunately, _____

_____ about their pet bird yet!)

11. I'm having a busy day. _____ with my

employees since 8:00 this morning. _____ already

_____ with 20 employees.

12. Professor Hawkins is really exhausted today. _____

lectures since 9:00 this morning. _____ already _____ two

lectures, and he has to give another one in a few minutes.

G. A NEW LIFE

Toshi has been living in a small town in Japan all his life. His father just got a job in the United States, and Toshi and his family are going to live there. Toshi's life is going to be very different in the United States.

1. He's going to live in a big city.
2. He's going to take English lessons.
3. He's going to shop in American supermarkets.
4. He's going to eat American food.
5. He's going to . . . .

Toshi is a little nervous because:

1. _____*He's never lived in a big city*_____ before.
2. _____ before.
3. _____ before.
4. _____ before.
5. _____ before.

Toshi's cousins have been living in the United States for many years. They'll be able to help him because:

1. _____*They've been living in a big city*_____ for years.
2. _____ for years.
3. _____ for years.
4. _____ for years.
5. _____ for years.

Toshi's cousins tell him he shouldn't worry. They're sure he'll enjoy his new life in the United States very much.

H.   YOU DECIDE: *A NEW LIFE*

. . . . has been living in . . . . all her life. Now she's

going to move to . . . . Her life is going to be very different in
(your city)

. . . .
(your city)

1.   She's going to . . . .

2.   She's going to . . . .

3.   She's going to . . . .

4.   She's going to . . . .

5.   She's going to . . . .

_____ is a little nervous because:

1.   She's never _____ before.

2.   She's never _____ before.

3.   She's never _____ before.

4.   She's never _____ before.

5.   She's never _____ before.

. . . . (has/have) been living in _____ for many years
and will be able to help her because:

1.   _____ for years.

2.   _____ for years.

3.   _____ for years.

4.   _____ for years.

5.   _____ for years.

_____ shouldn't worry. I'm sure she'll enjoy her new life in _____

_____ very much.

I.   YOU DECIDE: *ASKING FOR A RAISE*

A.   Mr. Harris. Could I speak with you for a few minutes?

B.   Of course. Please sit down.

A.   Mr. Harris, I've been thinking. I've been working here at The . . . .

Company (for/since) . . . . I've worked very hard, and I've done a lot of

things here. For example, I've . . . . , I've . . . .

. . . . , and I've been . . . . (for/since)

. . . .

B.   That's true, Mr. Jones. And we're happy with your work.

A.   Thank you, Mr. Harris. As I was saying, I know I've done a very good job here and I really think I

should get a raise. I haven't had a raise (for/since) . . . .

. . . .

B.   . . . .

. . . .

. . . .

A.   . . . .

. . . .

. . . .

J.   LISTEN

Listen and fill in the missing words.

1. I've been _____ a lot of _____ recently, but I _____ _____ any that I

   really liked. What good movies _____ you _____ _____ month? _____ you

   _____ _____ any movies _____ _____?

2. Ted _____ _____ _____ very long, but he _____ whenever he

   _____. _____ already _____ downtown three times _____ _____, and I

   think _____ _____ downtown again this afternoon.

3. Sheila _____ _____ a _____ _____ photographs of her _____. _____

   _____ _____ photographs of _____ for _____. I think _____ _____

   photographs are the _____ ones _____ _____ _____.

4. Mrs. Warren _____ _____ _____ piano lessons this _____, and

   _____ _____ another lesson _____ a _____ _____. After that,

   _____ _____ _____ _____ any more lessons _____.

5. Bobby _____ _____ his dinner tonight because _____ already _____ dessert.

   Bobby _____ _____ _____ very well _____ his grandmother _____

   _____ a large box of _____ _____ week.

CHECK-UP TEST: Chapters 4-6

A.   Complete the sentences with the present perfect.

Ex. (do)   a. Stuart ___has___ already ___done___ his homework.

   (read)   b. I ___haven't read___ the newspaper yet.

(go)   1. Max and his brother _____ already _____ to the beach.

(take)   2. Diane _____ her piano lesson yet.

(write)   3. I _____ to my parents yet.

(eat)   4. My wife and I _____ already _____ dinner.

(pay)   5. You _____ your electric bill yet.

(leave)   6. Herbert _____ already _____ for work.

B.   Complete the questions.

1. _____ her new necklace   Yes, she has. She wore it yesterday.
   yet?

2. _____ home yet?   Yes, they have. They got home a little while
                                                    ago.

3. _____ to the   No, I haven't. I'm going to speak to her this
   doctor yet?   afternoon.

4. _____ the new   Yes, he has. He saw it last week.
   movie at the Central Theater yet?

5. _____ ever _____ in a   Yes, I have. I ran in a marathon last spring.
   marathon?

6. _____ ever _____ in an   Yes, she has. She flew to Madrid two years ago.
   airplane?

C.   Complete the sentences.

Ex. a. I'm very tired. _____*I've been*_____ tired since I got up this morning.

    b. Susan is reading. _____*She's been reading*_____ since noon.

1. It's cloudy. _____ cloudy since yesterday.

2. We're studying. _____ since 3:00.

3. My son has a toothache. _____ a toothache since early this morning.

4. My children are arguing. _____ all morning.

5. Jane is sleeping. _____ since 8:00 last night.

6. My sister and I are interested in Italian. _____ interested in Italian since we visited
   Rome.

7. I'm baking cookies. _____ cookies for several hours.

8. Richard knows how to ski. _____ how to ski since he was very young.

D. Complete the answers.

> for   since

1. How long has your father been working at the post office?

_____ 1975.

2. How long has your daughter been married?

_____ three years.

3. How long have you and your friend been waiting?

_____ an hour.

4. How long has it been raining?

_____ Friday.

5. How long have you wanted to be an actress?

_____ I was a teenager.

E. Complete the sentences.

1. Ted owns a car. _____ a car since last year.

Before that, _____ a motorcycle.

2. I'm a mechanic. _____ a mechanic since 1980.

Before that, _____ a plumber.

3. My neighbors have a cat. _____ a cat since last winter.

Before that, _____ a dog.

4. My daughter likes jazz. _____ jazz for the past few months.

Before that, _____ rock and roll.

LISTENING TEST

Listen and fill in the missing words.

1. A. Timothy _____ _____ _____ since _____ _____ up. _____
    already _____ more than ten pages. Who's he _____ _____?

   B. He's probably _____ to _____ girlfriend. He _____ _____ to _____
       _____ weeks.

2. Mrs. Morgan _____ _____ three violin lessons this _____, but she _____
    _____ _____ any more lessons this afternoon. She's _____ _____
    a lot of lessons _____, and she's _____ tired.

A. WHAT DO THEY {ENJOY DOING / LIKE TO DO} ?

enjoy _____ ing	
like to _____	_____ ing

1. I don't enjoy ____*going*____ to the doctor, but I went yesterday for my annual checkup.

2. Mrs. McDonald is very energetic. She ____*likes to*____ lift weights. She thinks that
____*lifting*____ weights is good exercise.

3. William _____ baking bread when he has free time.

4. I _____ swim after a busy day. In my opinion, _____ is a good way to relax.

5. My husband doesn't _____ working late at the office, but sometimes he has to.

6. My wife and I ski during the winter, and in the summer we _____ to play tennis.

7. Bob doesn't _____ give blood, but he knows that _____ blood is a good thing to do.

8. Roberta doesn't _____ lying in the sun because she's afraid she'll get a sunburn.

9. My wife _____ jog five miles every day. She thinks _____ is the best exercise in the world.

10. I _____ go to parties. I think _____ is a good way to meet people.

11. School is O.K., but my brother and I don't really _____ doing homework.

12. Alice _____ eat rich desserts, but her doctor thinks that _____ rich desserts is bad for her heart.

13. Mary doesn't really enjoy _____ her apartment, but she tries to clean it once a week.

14. My little brother doesn't _____ go to bed at eight o'clock. He thinks _____ to bed at eight o'clock is too early.

15. My husband and I get up early during the week, but on weekends we enjoy _____ late.

16. I really want to learn English, but I don't _____ study.

68

B. YOU DECIDE: *WHAT'S THE REASON?*

1. Fred is happy he works in a restaurant because he enjoys . . . . *baking fancy desserts (or)* . . . .
. . . . *eating lots of good food (or) cooking different kinds of foods.* . . . .

2. Mrs. Watson is sorry she has ten children because she hates. . . . .

. . . .

3. Mr. Davis is glad he's a teacher because he likes. . . . .

. . . .

4. I'm sorry I'm a secretary because I can't stand . . . .

. . . .

5. Michael is glad he's going to college next year because he enjoys . . . .

. . . .

6. Martin enjoys living in Honolulu because he likes . . . .

. . . .

7. Diane wants to be a carpenter because she enjoys. . . . .

. . . .

8. Andy hates living in the city because he can't stand . . . .

. . . .

9. Gloria is very happy she's a Hollywood actress because she enjoys . . . .

. . . .

10. Marion is glad she knows how to speak English because she likes . . . .

. . . . : . . . .

C. MY ENERGETIC GRANDMOTHER

A. Your grandmother is a very energetic woman.

B. She sure is!

A. When did she start _____ tennis?

B. Believe it or not, she learned _____ tennis when she was sixty years old!

A. That's fantastic! Does she practice _____ tennis very often?

B. Yes, she does. She practices every day.

A. What else does she enjoy doing?

B. She enjoys . . . ., she enjoys . . . ., and she also enjoys . . . .

A. I hope I have that much energy when I'm her age!

D. I CAN'T STAND IT!

I spoke to my friend Roberta last weekend, and she talked a lot about tap dancing. Ever since she started to tap dance a few months ago, that's all she ever talks about! I never see her any more because she practices tap dancing all the time. And whenever I talk to her on the phone, tap dancing is the only thing she wants to talk about! (She thinks that everybody should learn to tap dance.)

I can't stand it! I don't ever want to hear another word about tap dancing!

Now YOU tell about somebody.

I spoke to my friend . . . . last weekend, and . . . . talked a lot about . . . . Ever since . . . .

. . . .

. . . .

. . . .

. . . .

. . . .

. . . .

E. YOU DECIDE: *WHAT'S LUCY GOING TO DO?*

A. Hello, Lucy. How are you? I haven't seen you in a long time. What have you been doing?

B. . . . .

A. Oh. And what have you decided to do after you finish studying English?

B. I've decided . . . .

A. Really? You're going to move to the United States? That's wonderful! What are you going to do there?

B. I'm considering . . . .

. . . .

A. Don't you think that . . . . will be difficult?

B. Oh, no. Not at all.

A. Have you considered . . . . ?

B. Yes, I have. But I've decided not to because. . . . .

. . . .

. . . .

A. And where have you decided to live?

B. I'm thinking about . . . .

A. Why do you want to live there?

B. . . . .

. . . .

A. Well, Lucy. Good luck. Let's get together sometime before you leave.

B. O.K. Good-bye.

A. Good-bye.

F. PROBLEMS

1. I'm very worried about my son. He keeps on ___eating___ junk food. I tell him that junk food is bad for his teeth,

   but he doesn't listen to me. He really should begin _____ more fruits and vegetables.

2. Linda speaks so softly in class. She really should

   begin _____ louder. No one can hear her at all.

3. If my neighbor's son doesn't stop _____ his violin at four o'clock in the morning, I'm going to have to complain to the landlord. He really should start

   _____ his violin during the day.

4. Maybe I shouldn't continue _____ basketball twice a day. I really like basketball, but I'm afraid I might hurt my back if I keep on

   _____ so often.

5. I've got to stop _____ late at the office

   every night. If I don't quit _____ late,

   my family will start _____ angry at me.

6. I'm really upset. My husband and his friends have started

   _____ a lot lately. I'm afraid if they

   keep on _____, we'll have to stop

   _____ money on movies and vacations.

7. Do you think I should continue _____ English? I'm not a very good student. My friends tell me

I should keep on _____ English. According

to them, if I quit _____ English now, I won't be able to speak it when I travel.

8. Harvey has got to stop _____ so fast and

start _____ more carefully. _____ fast isn't safe.

9. Mr. Smith! When are you going to begin _____

more neatly? If you don't stop _____ so sloppily, I'm going to have to fire you.

10. My boyfriend George is so clumsy. When we go dancing

at the discotheque, he keeps on _____ on my feet. I like to dance with him, but if he doesn't

stop _____ on my feet, I'm never going to dance with him again.

11. I should quit _____ scary TV programs

before I go to bed. If I keep on _____

scary TV programs, I'll keep on _____ nightmares.

12. Should I stop _____ out with

Doris and start _____ out with Jane?

Or should I keep on _____ out with Doris and go out with Jane, too? I really can't decide because I like them both!

G. LISTEN

Listen and put a circle around the correct answer.

1. a. listen to jazz.
    b. (circled) going to the symphony.

2. a. eating junk food.
    b. to pay our bills late.

3. a. to sew.
    b. baking bread.

4. a. to ski.
    b. figure skating.

5. a. to buy a new TV.
    b. taking a vacation.

6. a. moving to my own apartment.
    b. to ask for a raise.

7. a. to go back to college?
    b. finding a new job?

8. a. to eat candy.
    b. having so much ice cream.

9. a. making mistakes?
    b. to go to bed after midnight?

10. a. to worry so much.
    b. smoking cigarettes.

11. a. get a good night's sleep.
    b. playing chess.

12. a. going to the dentist.
    b. see the doctor.

13. a. taking violin lessons?
    b. study the piano?

14. a. to review his history lesson.
    b. clean his apartment.

15. a. studying astronomy.
    b. teach a computer course.

16. a. to live at home with your parents.
    b. going to school for the rest of your life.

H. WHAT DOES IT MEAN?

Put a circle around the correct answer.

1. Harry is going to the health club this afternoon.
    a. He has a doctor's appointment.
    b. (circled) He's going to exercise.
    c. He's going to have a checkup.

2. Peter and Helen are engaged.
    a. They don't know each other.
    b. They're married.
    c. They're going to get married.

3. My wife has a fever.
    a. I'm glad to hear that.
    b. How long has she been feeling sick?
    c. Do you think I can borrow it?

4. Carmen has made plans for the summer.
   a. She knows what she's going to do this summer.
   b. She hasn't decided what she's going to do this summer.
   c. She's made a lot of new summer clothes.

5. What's your present address?
   a. Where do you live now?
   b. Where are you going to move?
   c. Where did you live when you were young?

6. My dog Rover has a big appetite.
   a. He sleeps a lot.
   b. He eats a lot.
   c. He looks terrible.

7. My mother is going to mend my shirt.
   a. She's going to wash my shirt.
   b. She's going to give my shirt to someone.
   c. She's going to fix my shirt.

8. I'm going to ask for a raise.
   a. You should speak to your boss.
   b. You should speak to your landlord.
   c. You should speak to your teacher.

9. I was standing in line.
   a. I was the only person there.
   b. There were ten people in front of me.
   c. Everybody liked my pictures.

10. Paul is a teenager.
    a. He's in high school.
    b. He just retired.
    c. He's ten years old.

11. My Uncle George has a Greek accent.
    a. He wears it all the time.
    b. He bought it when he was in Greece.
    c. Everybody knows he's from Greece.

12. Dr. Jones has a lot of patients.
    a. He never gets angry.
    b. He's a very popular doctor.
    c. I know. He never gets sick.

A. BEFORE

1. Mr. and Mrs. Hardy couldn't stop talking about their grandson last night.

    They (visit) __had__ just __visited__ him the week before.

2. I'm sorry I couldn't help you yesterday, but I (get) _____ just _____ back from my vacation, and I had a lot to do.

3. Eric had to study all weekend because he (do) _____ _____ very badly on his history examination.

4. My husband invited some friends for dessert, and he forgot to tell me. Fortunately, I (bake) _____

    just _____ an apple pie a few hours before they arrived.

5. Mrs. Martin was very tired yesterday morning because she (give) _____ _____ a big party the night before.

6. I didn't buy any more milk today because we (buy) _____ just _____ some yesterday.

7. Jeffrey looked wonderful when I saw him last Tuesday. He (go) _____ _____ on a diet the week before.

8. We stopped driving at 10:00 because we (drive) _____ already _____ 400 miles, and we wanted to rest.

9. Timothy was crying when I visited him yesterday. He (hurt) _____ just _____ himself.

10. Mr. and Mrs. Schultz couldn't buy the record player they wanted because they (spend) _____

    _____ all their money on their vacation.

11. When I got up this morning, my wife (leave) _____ already _____ for work.

12. Sheila couldn't lend me her English book because she (lose) _____ _____ it.

13. Donald looked terrible when I saw him. His clothes were dirty, and he (grow) _____

    _____ a beard.

14. Katherine didn't sleep well last night because she (eat) _____ _____ a large piece of pizza before she went to bed.

76

B. LATE FOR EVERYTHING

Joe Richards was very upset yesterday. He didn't get up until 10 a.m., and he was late for EVERYTHING all day.

French class begins at 11:00.

1. He got to his French class at 11:30.

   It ___*had*___ already ___*begun.*___

Mrs. Wilson is giving a science test at 2:00.

3. He got to science class at 3:00.

   Mrs. Wilson _____ already _____ the test.

Professor Dupont's lecture on modern French poetry starts at 4:30.

5. He got to the lecture at 5:00.

   It _____ already _____.

| Dear Joe,
We'll be arriving on the 6:00 plane. |
| :--- |

7. He got to the airport at 6:15.

   His aunt and uncle _____ already

   _____.

| Dear Joe,
Let's have an early lunch. I have to go back to work at 1:00. |
| :--- |

2. He got to the restaurant at 1:30.

   His friend _____ already _____ back to work.

| Dear Joe,
I'll be leaving at 3:30. Hope to see you before then. |
| :--- |

4. He got to his friend's house at 4:00.

   His friend _____ already _____.

The library is going to close at 5:00 today.

6. He got to the library at 5:30.

   It _____ already _____.

Mary Richards and Edward Thompson will be getting married on April 19th at 8:00.

8. He got to the church at 9:00.

   His cousin Mary _____ already

   _____ married.

C. TOM TOUGH

Tom Tough got out of jail yesterday. He had been in jail for ten long years. Before Tom went to jail, he enjoyed:

1. visiting his friends

2. driving his motorcycle

3. going bowling

He also enjoyed:

4. ....

5. ....

6. ....

7. ....

8. ....

Yesterday was the happiest day of Tom's life. He did all the things he hadn't done in a long time.

1. _____*He visited his friends*_____ again. _____*He hadn't visited them*_____ in ten years.

2. _____ again. _____ in ten years.

3. _____ again. _____ in ten years.

4. _____ again. _____ in ten years.

5. _____ again. _____ in ten years.

6. _____ again. _____ in ten years.

7. _____ again. _____ in ten years.

8. _____ again. _____ in ten years.

78

D. WORKING HARD

Linda was very busy after school
yesterday.

3:00	write an English composition
4:00	study for my math examination
5:00	review my French lessons
6:00	read the next history lesson

What was she doing at 4:00?

1. _____ *She was studying for*

_____ *her math examination.*

What had she already done?

2. _____ *She had already written an English composition.* _____

What hadn't she done yet?

3. _____ *She hadn't reviewed her French lessons yet.* _____

4. _____

Sharon and Roberta were very busy this
morning getting ready for the marathon.

8:00	go jogging
9:00	swim across the pool 100 times
10:00	lift weights
11:00	take a karate lesson

What were they doing at 10:00?

5. _____

What had they already done?

6. _____

7. _____

What hadn't they done yet?

8. _____

Bobby spent all yesterday afternoon
making Christmas gifts.

1:00	draw a picture for my mother
2:00	build a birdhouse for my cousins
3:00	write a story for my father
4:00	knit a sweater for Rover

What was he doing at 2:00?

9. _____

_____

What had he already done?

10. _____

What hadn't he done yet?

11. _____

12. _____

E.   A VERY SHY PERSON

My friend Walter is a very shy person.

1. _____*He had been going*_____ out with his girlfriend Alice for five years before he asked her to marry him.

2. _____ in his apartment house for two years before he ever spoke to any of his neighbors.

3. _____ the piano for twenty years before he ever played in front of his family.

4. _____ poetry for ten years before he read his poems to any of his friends.

5. _____ French for eight years before he ever spoke it with anybody.

6. And _____ at the bank for twelve years before he asked for a raise.

My friend Walter is the shyest person I know.

F. WHAT ARE THEY SAYING?

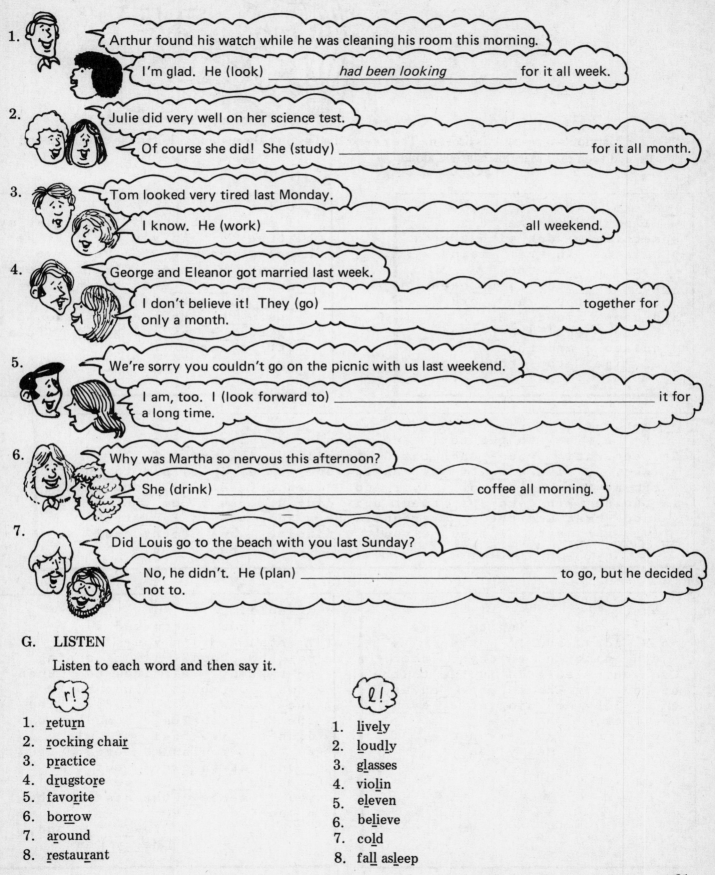

1. Arthur found his watch while he was cleaning his room this morning.

   I'm glad. He (look) _____*had been looking*_____ for it all week.

2. Julie did very well on her science test.

   Of course she did! She (study) _____ for it all month.

3. Tom looked very tired last Monday.

   I know. He (work) _____ all weekend.

4. George and Eleanor got married last week.

   I don't believe it! They (go) _____ together for only a month.

5. We're sorry you couldn't go on the picnic with us last weekend.

   I am, too. I (look forward to) _____ it for a long time.

6. Why was Martha so nervous this afternoon?

   She (drink) _____ coffee all morning.

7. Did Louis go to the beach with you last Sunday?

   No, he didn't. He (plan) _____ to go, but he decided not to.

G. LISTEN

Listen to each word and then say it.

r!

1. retu<u>r</u>n
2. <u>r</u>ocking chai<u>r</u>
3. p<u>r</u>actice
4. d<u>r</u>ugsto<u>r</u>e
5. favo<u>r</u>ite
6. bo<u>rr</u>ow
7. a<u>r</u>ound
8. <u>r</u>estau<u>r</u>ant

l!

1. live<u>l</u>y
2. <u>l</u>oud<u>l</u>y
3. g<u>l</u>asses
4. vio<u>l</u>in
5. e<u>l</u>even
6. be<u>l</u>ieve
7. co<u>l</u>d
8. fa<u>ll</u> as<u>l</u>eep

81

H.   MA_Y _OU'S B_OKEN TYPEW_ITER

Marylou's typewriter is broken. The r's and the l's don't always work. Fill in the missing r's and l's, and then read Marylou's letters aloud.

1.

```
__obert,
   I'm af__aid the__e's
something w__ong with the
__adiato__ in the __iving
__oom.  A__so, the
__ef__ige__ator is b__oken.
I ca___ed the __and__ord
and comp__ained.  He'___
t__y to __epair both the
__adiato__ and the
__ef__ige__ato__ tomo__ow.
            Ma__y__ou
```

2.

```
__ouise,
   I'm te__ibly wo__ied about my
b__othe__ __ar__y's health.  He
hasn't been fee__ing ve__y we___
__ecent__y.  Acco__ding to Docto__
__arson, __a__y is having
p__ob__ems with his b__ood
p__essu__e.  He __eal__y should
t__y to __e__ax and take __ife a
__itt__e easie__.
                  Ma__y__ou
```

3.

```
__oger,
   He__e's how to get to I__ene's house.  D__ive a__ong Cent__al
St__eet unti__ you __each the G__eenville __ib__ary.  Tu__n
__ight.  D__ive a __itt__e __onger (one mo__e mi__e) and tu__n
__eft at the co__ner of __iver and G__een St__eets.  I__ene lives
in the da__k b__own apa__tment bui__ding ac__oss f__om the
__aund__omat and the p__ayground.  He__ add__ess is Fou__teen
__ive__ St__eet.  I'm su__e you'___ find he__ apa__tment easi__y.
                                                  Ma__y__ou
```

4.

```
__osa,
   I'___ be f__ying to __ome
on F__iday, and I'___ be
__etu__ning th__ee days __ater.
Can you p__ease d__ive me to the
ai__po__t?  The p__ane __eaves
on F__iday mo__ning at e__even
o'c__ock.
            A___ my __ove,
            Ma__y__ou
```

5.

```
A__nold,
   Can you __ecommend a
__estau__ant in you__
neighbo__hood?  I'm p__anning
to take my __elatives to __unch
tomo___ow, but I'm not su__e
whe__e.  We've a___eady t__ied
the Eng__ish Tea __oom, but we
didn't __ike thei__ f__uit
sa__ad.  You and G__ego__y had
__unch at an exce__ent
__estau__ant __ast week.  Do
you __emembe__ the name of the
p__ace?
            You__ f__iend,
            Ma__y__ou
```

82

I. LISTEN

Listen to each sentence. Put a circle around the appropriate answer.

Ex. a. She can't find it anywhere.
   b. Where can they be?
   (c.) We can't hear her at all.

1. a. I hope he feels better soon.
   b. What happened? Did you twist it?
   c. How are your cousins?

2. a. Did you take a lot of photographs?
   b. I'm glad you didn't fall and hurt yourself.
   c. That's too bad. I know you were looking forward to it.

3. a. I know. He's missed all his tests.
   b. I know. He's been doing very poorly.
   c. I know. He hasn't taken any tests this year.

4. a. How many miles did you travel?
   b. Isn't flying in airplanes dangerous?
   c. Did you enjoy yourselves?

5. a. What a shame! She won't be able to sing.
   b. What a shame! She won't be able to knit.
   c. What a shame! She won't be able to walk.

6. a. No. We work for different companies.
   b. No. She's my aunt.
   c. Yes. She's my mother's cousin.

7. a. Did you see anything interesting?
   b. Did you buy a new kitchen window?
   c. Did you get everything you needed?

8. a. Was it a very bad accident?
   b. Do you know anybody who can repair it?
   c. How long had you been going out together?

9. a. He's having problems with his teeth.
   b. That's O.K. We all make mistakes.
   c. He's having problems with his feet.

10. a. I think so. She's been working very hard.
    b. I think so. The airport isn't very crowded.
    c. I hope so. She wears them all the time.

11. a. We wrote about politics.
    b. We talked about modern art.
    c. We read about computer technology.

12. a. No. Where was he going?
    b. No. I didn't see the bus stop.
    c. No, I didn't. But I heard the music.

13. a. He's going to have a party.
    b. He's going to go on vacation.
    c. He received a lot of presents on his birthday.

14. a. When did you learn how to sew?
    b. Who are you giving it to?
    c. Would you like to talk about it?

15. a. Poor Patty. She's always sick.
    b. Poor Patty. She needs a new pair of boots.
    c. She's too shy.

16. a. I like you, too.
    b. You don't have anything to be jealous about.
    c. What are you going to send me?

A. Complete the sentences with the appropriate verb form.

(eat)   1. Why do you keep on _____ junk food?

(smoke)   2. My mother thinks _____ is bad for my health.

(move)   3. I've decided _____ to a new apartment.

(swim)   4. Jim practices _____ every day.

(dance)   5. _____ is a good way to relax.

(play)   6. Where did your sister learn _____ the guitar so well?

(talk)   7. Please stop _____. I'm trying to sleep!

(get up)   8. Sally thinks _____ early is a good way to start the day.

B.   Complete the sentences using the past perfect tense.

Ex. (go)   The jazz concert last night was wonderful. I _____ *hadn't gone* _____ to a jazz
             concert since last summer.

   (start)   By the time Anita got to church, the wedding ___ *had* ___ already ___ *started.* ___

(speak)   1. I had dinner with some Spanish friends last night. I enjoyed myself because I

              _____ Spanish in a long time.

(do)   2. By the time Susan's father got home from work, she _____ already _____
              her homework and was ready to play chess with him.

(leave)   3. George was upset. By the time he got to the train, it _____ already _____.

(write)   4. I wrote a long letter to my grandparents last night because I _____
              to them in several months.

(give)   5. Peter didn't give blood last January because he _____ blood three
              months before.

(wear)   6. I wore the dress my husband gave me to the party last night because I

              _____ it in a long time.

(eat)   7. I ate a piece of chocolate cake last night and felt terrible about it. I

              _____ a rich dessert since I started my diet.

C. Complete the sentences using the past perfect continuous tense.

Ex. (study)   Shirley was glad she did well on her geography exam. She ___*had been studying*___ for it for days.

(practice)   1. Steve lost the tennis match this afternoon. He was upset because he

_____ hard for the past few months.

(plan)   2. Mr. and Mrs. Martin didn't go on their vacation because they got sick. They were sorry

because they _____ their trip for months.

(look forward)   3. I'm disappointed you had to cancel your party last weekend. I_____

_____ to it for a long time.

(argue)   4. Ann and Jeff broke up last night. They _____ with each other for the past several weeks.

D. Listen and put a circle around the correct answer.

Ex. (a.) take photographs.
    b. painting portraits.

1. a. eating so much ice cream.
   b. smoke so many cigarettes.

2. a. to take out Betty.
   b. marrying Linda.

3. a. to move into an apartment.
   b. buying a house.

4. a. taking piano lessons.
   b. study the violin.

5. a. to make her own clothes.
   b. working in her garden.

6. a. teach history.
   b. working at the university.

A. WHAT ARE THEY SAYING?

1.  Did you pick up Rover at the vet today?

    No. I didn't _____*pick him up.*_____ I thought YOU did.

2. A. When did the children turn on the TV?

    B. They _____ three hours ago. They've been watching it all afternoon.

3. A. Has Paul filled out his income tax form yet?

    B. Yes, he has. He _____ last week.

4. A. Where can I hang up my hat and coat?

    B. You can _____ in the closet next to mine.

5. Did Sharon bring back her library books yesterday?

    B. No, she didn't. She's going to _____ today.

6. A. When are you going to throw out these old souvenirs from our trip to Rome?

    B. I'm never going to _____. They'll always be very special to me.

7. A. Have your parents picked out their new car yet?

    B. Yes, they have. They _____ yesterday.

8. A. Has Julia put away her wedding gown?

    B. No, she hasn't. She's going to _____ after she brings it back from the cleaner's.

9. A. Did Charlie call up his mother to wish her "Happy Birthday"?

    B. No. He didn't _____. He forgot it was her birthday!

86

B. WHAT ARE THEY SAYING?

bring back	put away	take out
call up	put on	turn off
hand in	take off	turn on

1. Why are you putting your pajamas _____on?_____ It's only eight o'clock in the evening.

Oh! I'm _____putting them on_____ because I thought it was eleven o'clock. I think my watch is broken.

2. When are you going to hand _____ your English composition?

I'm going to _____ tomorrow morning before class. I have to write it tonight.

3. Have you put your school books _____ for the summer?

I sure have. I _____ last week. I don't want to see them again until next September.

4. Why don't you take _____ your hat and coat? It's warm in here.

I'll _____ in a few minutes. I'm still a little cold.

5. You haven't called your Uncle Henry _____ recently.

I know. When I _____ last month, he talked for more than two hours. I really hate long telephone calls.

6. Did you turn your heat _____ last night?

Yes, I did. I _____ for the first time this winter. It was a very cold night.

7. When are the neighbors going to turn their record player _____? It's after midnight!

I don't know. But if they don't _____ soon, I'm going to call the landlord.

8. Do you think Marylou will bring her boyfriend _____ to the house after the soccer game?

I don't know. Maybe she'll _____. I really want to meet him.

C. WHAT ARE THEY SAYING?

cross out	look up	turn down
do over	think over	use up
give back	throw* away *(throw, threw, thrown)	write down

1.

   What's the matter with the radio, Grandma? Is it broken?

   No, it isn't. I _____*turned it off*_____ because I couldn't stand listening to that loud rock and roll music.

2. A. Are you going to accept your new job offer?

   B. I don't know. I'll have to _____ carefully.

3. A. What's Mr. and Mrs. Warren's telephone number?

   B. I'm not sure. Why don't you _____ in the telephone book?

4. A. Did Alice go out with Fred last night?

   B. No, she didn't. She had to _____ because she already had a date with somebody else.

5. A. Do our neighbors still have the keys to our house?

   B. No, they don't. They _____ after our vacation.

6. A. What's Donald's new address?

   B. I'm not sure. But I know I _____ somewhere.

7. A. Mrs. Smith really liked the English composition I handed in.

   B. I envy you. You won't have to _____ for homework tomorrow.

8. A. Where's the sugar?

   B. I'm sorry, but there isn't any. I _____ when I made that carrot cake last night.

9. A. Should I erase all these mistakes in my science homework?

   B. Why don't you just _____ ?

10.

    What did you do with this morning's newspaper?

    I _____. Didn't you already read it?

D. GETTING READY FOR A VACATION

Put a circle around the correct answer.

The Grant family is going to go on vacation today. Everyone in the family is excited because they're going to go skiing for two weeks. Here are some things they have to do before they leave.

What does Mr. Grant have to do?

1. He has to (drop off) / turn off their dog at a friend's house.

2. He has to take out / take off some money from the bank for their trip.

What does Mrs. Grant have to do?

3. She has to hang up / figure out the telephone and electric bills.

4. She has to put away / throw away the laundry.

5. She has to cross out / throw out some old newspapers and magazines and put on / pick up some new ones to read on the plane.

What do Lucy and Arthur have to do?

6. They have to take down / put on the Christmas decorations from last night's party.

7. They have to pick out / use up the clothes they'll need for the trip.

8. Lucy also has to hand in / give back the ice skates she borrowed from her friend.

9. And Arthur has to call up / hang up their hotel to say they'll be arriving late.

E. HOW ABOUT YOU?

You're going to go on vacation today. What do you have to do before you leave?

1. I have to _____ _____ my English homework. My teacher wants it before I leave.

2. I have to _____ _____ my apartment. It's very dirty.

3. I have to _____ _____ the clothes I left at the cleaner's. I'll need them for my trip.

4. I have to _____ _____ my vacation address and telephone number and give it to my neighbor.

5. I have to remember to _____ _____ a light in the living room so my apartment won't be dark.

6. Also, I have to. . . . .
    . . . .

F. WHAT SHOULD THEY DO?

call up	look up	put on	throw out	write down
do over	pick up	take down	turn off	
give back	put away	think over	use up	

1. A. The heat is on too high.

    B. Why don't you _____ *turn it off?* _____

90

2. A. I don't know the definition of this word.

   B. You really should _____.

3. A. We haven't talked to Uncle Fred on the telephone in months!

   B. You're right. Let's _____ today.

4. A. I can NEVER remember your address.

   B. It's 45 Main Street. Why don't you _____?

5. A. Believe it or not, it's summer and my skis are still in my car!

   B. Don't you think it's time to _____?

6. A. I don't know if we should hire Mr. Stevens or Mr. Sharp.

   B. It's a very difficult decision. Let's _____.

7. A. This English composition I just wrote is very boring.

   B. I know. Maybe you should _____.

8. A. It's March and my Christmas decorations are still up!

   B. They are?! Why don't you _____?

9. A. Aunt Gertrude is going to arrive at the bus station in a little while.

   B. Well, I guess we really should _____.

10. A. I still haven't returned my neighbor's screwdriver.

    B. You haven't? You borrowed it three months ago. Why don't you

       _____?

11. A. Do you want to see my new fur jacket?

    B. Sure. _____!

12. A. I'm very embarrassed. These are the worst photographs anyone has ever taken of me.

    B. Well, if they bother you that much, why don't you _____?

13. A. We still have half a bottle of soda. Should I buy some more?

    B. Don't bother. Let's _____ first.

G. COME UP WITH THE RIGHT ANSWER

call on	hear from	pick on
get along with	look through	run into
get over	look up to	take after

1. I _____*take after*_____ my mother. We're both athletic, we're both interested in music, and we both like to paint. I'm really glad I _____*take after her.*_____.

2. My wife and I have both had the flu this winter. I had it for only one week, but she had it for three. I think I _____ faster because I stayed home and took care of myself.

3. I'm so embarrassed. Professor Kendall _____ three times in class today, and I didn't know ANY of the answers. I've got to study harder.

4. I can't believe it! I _____ my old boyfriend in the drugstore yesterday afternoon. And then I _____ again last night at the movie theater!

5. I don't _____ my mother-in-law very well. We often disagree. All the other people in our family _____. Why can't I?

6. I haven't _____ my Uncle Bill in three weeks. I hope he's O.K. I usually _____ every week, and I always enjoy his letters. I really should call him up tonight.

7. Why does my big sister _____ so much? I try to be nice to her, but she bothers me all the time.

8. I really enjoyed _____ my old love letters last night. I hadn't _____ in a long time.

9. I really _____ my grandfather. He's honest, intelligent, and very kind. I hope someday when I'm a grandfather, my grandchildren will _____, too.

92

Listen to each sentence. Put a circle around the appropriate answer.

1. a. blue
    b. $15
    c. large

2. a. Fine, I'll buy it.
    b. Don't worry. We have larger ones.
    c. I know. It's very baggy.

3. a. Everything in the store is cheaper this week.
    b. Everything in the store is 20 cents less this week.
    c. The store isn't having a sale this week.

4. a. How many pairs of shoes did you use up?
    b. How many pairs of shoes did you put on?
    c. How many pairs of shoes did you buy?

5. a. Was it a bad accident?
    b. That's nice. You haven't seen him in a long time.
    c. Do you like to jog?

6. a. It's too hot in this room.
    b. It's too cold in this room.
    c. It's very windy.

7. a. He's always with her.
    b. They're both shy.
    c. His mother always arrives first.

8. a. He's taller than I am.
    b. I can never find him when I need him.
    c. I want to be like him.

9. a. I'm sure you enjoy it.
    b. I'm sure that bothers you.
    c. You're lucky she has a car.

10. a. Yes, I put it in the closet.
     b. Yes, I gave it to our neighbor.
     c. Yes, we had used it all up.

11. a. Are you enjoying your trip?
     b. I'm glad you're feeling better.
     c. What a shame! When are you going to call the doctor?

12. a. The music was very loud.
     b. Somebody had picked it up.
     c. I already had a date.

13. a. Yes, her brother in Chicago says she's fine.
     b. No, she hasn't written in a while.
     c. No, she has a very soft voice.

14. a. He didn't need it anymore.
     b. It was at the cleaner's.
     c. He found a suit he liked.

15. a. It was easy because the dentist's office is near his company.
     b. He had had a toothache.
     c. He was very careless.

16. a. If you don't hurry, he'll probably miss his plane.
     b. I hope he hasn't been waiting long.
     c. Did he fall down?

17. a. He turned it on when he came home.
     b. He forgot to take it to work.
     c. He wanted the house to be cool when he came home.

18. a. They often disagree with each other.
     b. She doesn't get upset with her brother.
     c. Mary thinks her brother is always right.

A. NOT THE ONLY ONE

1.

I can take a few days off next week.

So _____can I._____

2.

I hate to go shopping.

_____, too.

3.

I'm still getting ready.

So _____.

4.

I just missed my plane.

_____, too.

GATE 7

5.

I was terribly hungry this morning.

So _____.

YOUR DIET

6.

I'll be starting a new job next week.

So _____.

7.

I'm going to be late again.

_____, too.

BUS STOP

8.

I've been making a lot of mistakes recently.

So _____.

B. WHAT A COINCIDENCE!

A. Do you live near here?

B. Yes. I live on Summer Street.

A. Really? So ____do I.____ I live in the brown apartment building next to Alan's Hardware Store.

B. What a coincidence! _____, too. I guess we're neighbors. My name is Ellen Peterson.

A. I'm Cynthia Blake. Glad to meet you.

B. How long have you been living on Summer Street?

A. I just moved in yesterday.

B. What a coincidence! _____, too. And I've been VERY busy.

A. So _____. Moving into a new apartment isn't easy.

B. Where will you be working?

A. I'll be working at the WHAMMO Furniture Company.

B. I don't believe it! So _____. In fact, I'm going there right now.

A. _____, too. We can go together.

B. That'll be nice.

C. NOT THE ONLY ONE

neither/either

1. I wasn't listening to the teacher.

   I wasn't either.

2. I'm not feeling very well.

   Neither _____.

3. I don't see your wallet.

Neither _____.

4. I didn't get the raise I asked for.

_____ either.

5. I never study for English exams.

_____

6. I haven't skied in a long time.

_____

7. I can't stand working here.

_____

8. I'll never be a good typist.

_____

D. LISTEN: *COINCIDENCES*

Listen and complete the sentences.

1. So _____ *was I.*

2. _____ , too.

3. Neither _____.

4. _____ either.

5. So _____.

6. _____ , too.

7. _____ either.

8. So _____.

9. So _____.

10. _____ , too.

11. Neither _____.

12. _____ , too.

13. Neither _____.

14. So _____.

15. Neither _____.

96

E. WHAT ARE THEY SAYING?

so/too

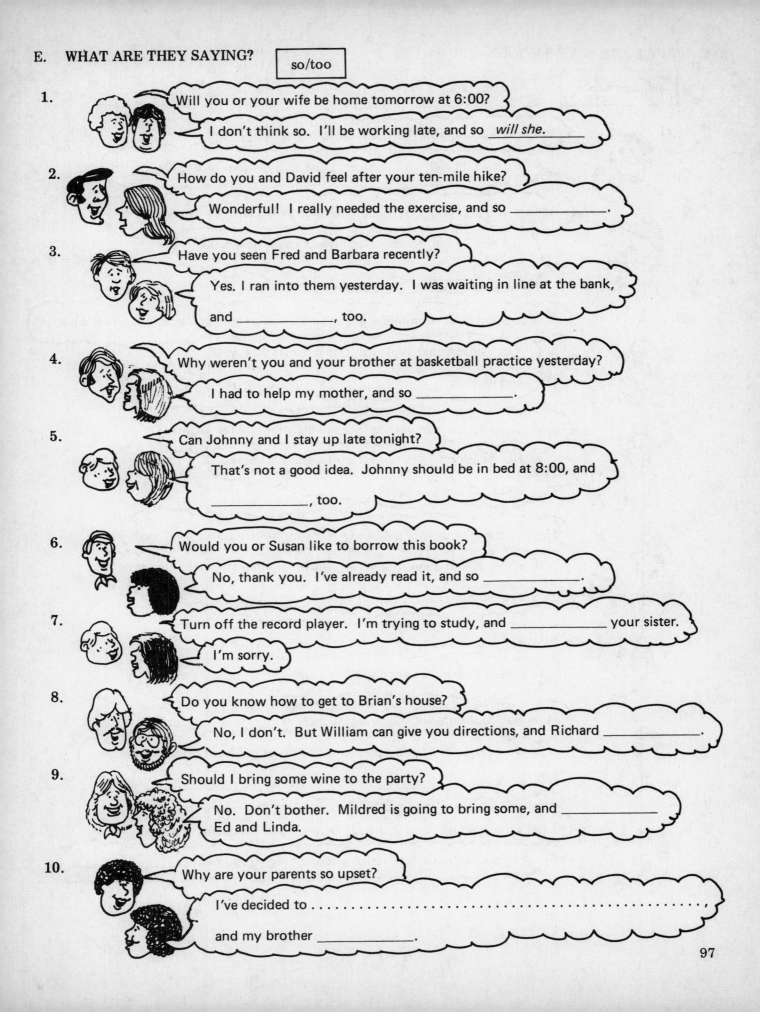

1. Will you or your wife be home tomorrow at 6:00?

   I don't think so. I'll be working late, and so _will she._

2. How do you and David feel after your ten-mile hike?

   Wonderful! I really needed the exercise, and so _____.

3. Have you seen Fred and Barbara recently?

   Yes. I ran into them yesterday. I was waiting in line at the bank,

   and _____, too.

4. Why weren't you and your brother at basketball practice yesterday?

   I had to help my mother, and so _____.

5. Can Johnny and I stay up late tonight?

   That's not a good idea. Johnny should be in bed at 8:00, and

   _____, too.

6. Would you or Susan like to borrow this book?

   No, thank you. I've already read it, and so _____.

7. Turn off the record player. I'm trying to study, and _____ your sister.

   I'm sorry.

8. Do you know how to get to Brian's house?

   No, I don't. But William can give you directions, and Richard _____.

9. Should I bring some wine to the party?

   No. Don't bother. Mildred is going to bring some, and _____
   Ed and Linda.

10. Why are your parents so upset?

    I've decided to . . . . ,

    and my brother _____.

F. WHAT ARE THEY SAYING?

neither/either

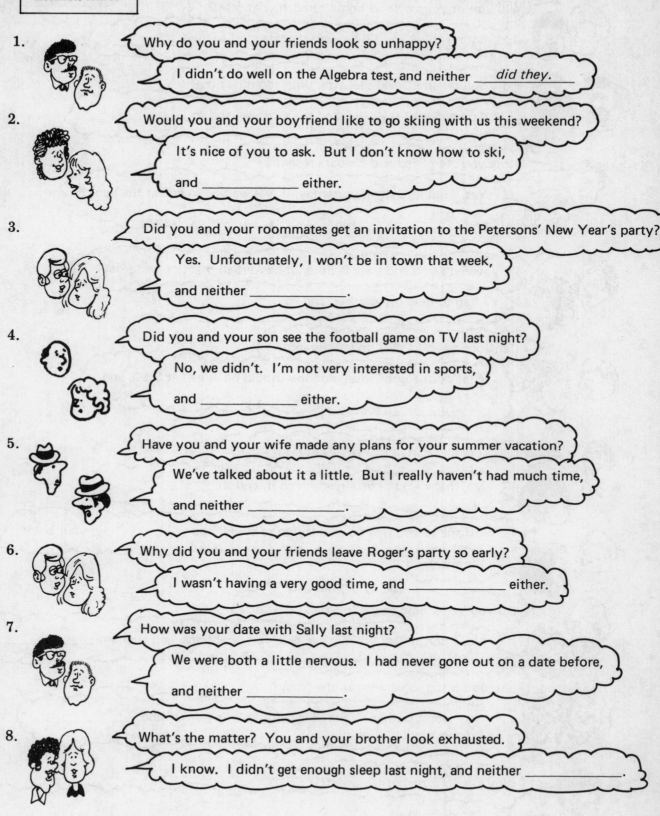

1. Why do you and your friends look so unhappy?

   I didn't do well on the Algebra test, and neither _____did they._____

2. Would you and your boyfriend like to go skiing with us this weekend?

   It's nice of you to ask. But I don't know how to ski,

   and _____ either.

3. Did you and your roommates get an invitation to the Petersons' New Year's party?

   Yes. Unfortunately, I won't be in town that week,

   and neither _____ .

4. Did you and your son see the football game on TV last night?

   No, we didn't. I'm not very interested in sports,

   and _____ either.

5. Have you and your wife made any plans for your summer vacation?

   We've talked about it a little. But I really haven't had much time,

   and neither _____ .

6. Why did you and your friends leave Roger's party so early?

   I wasn't having a very good time, and _____ either.

7. How was your date with Sally last night?

   We were both a little nervous. I had never gone out on a date before,

   and neither _____ .

8. What's the matter? You and your brother look exhausted.

   I know. I didn't get enough sleep last night, and neither _____ .

9.

Should I make dinner now?

There's no hurry. I'm not very hungry, and the children _____.

10.

Is the TV still broken?

I'm afraid it is. I haven't been able to fix it,

and _____ your father.

G. WHAT ARE THEY SAYING?

so/too/neither/either

1.

How did you and your cousins learn to speak Spanish so well?

I lived in Mexico City when I was young, and | *so did they.* | *they did, too.*

2.

Did you and Rita enjoy the concert last night?

Not really. I couldn't hear the music very well,

and _____.

3.

Can you and your sister go to the movies tonight?

I don't think so. I haven't done my homework yet,

and _____.

4.

You and Walter really should order the cheesecake. It's delicious.

I'm sure it is. But Walter can't eat rich desserts,

and _____.

5.

Why don't you and your husband stay a little longer? The party has just begun.

I'm afraid we can't. I have to get up early tomorrow morning,

and _____.

6.

Why aren't you and Michael good friends any more?

I'm in love with Julia, and _____.

99

H. LISTEN: *DIFFERENCES*

Listen and complete the sentences.

1. but you ____*didn't.*____

2. but I _____.

3. but my wife _____.

4. but Maria _____.

5. but my roommate _____.

6. but my children _____.

7. but I _____.

8. but our teacher _____.

9. but my daughter _____.

10. but I _____.

11. but William _____.

12. but my husband _____.

13. but you _____.

14. but my friends _____.

15. but the other driver _____.

I. OUR FAMILY

1. My father isn't very athletic, but my uncle ____*is.*____ He enjoys ____*going*____ to the health club and _____ exercises.

2. I can't play chess at all, but my sister _____. She's been _____ chess since she _____ six years old.

3. When we were young, my brother and sister were allergic to eggs, but I _____. Fortunately, I've always _____ able to eat everything.

4. My mother has lived here all her life, but her parents _____. They've been _____ in this country _____ forty years. Before that, they _____ in France.

5. My grandparents sometimes speak to us in French, but my mother _____. She _____ _____ French to anyone in a long time.

6. I'm not interested in math, but my mother _____. She likes _____ figure _____ very difficult math problems.

7. I don't have a very good voice, but my father _____. He enjoys _____ in the church _____.

8. I'll be going to college next year, but my sister _____. She _____ finished high school yet.

100

9. I've always done well in school, but my brother _____. He's never _____ a very good student.

10. I'm usually neat, but my sister _____. She never hangs _____ her clothes or _____ away her books.

11. My sister studied Spanish last year, but my brother _____. He studied Portuguese instead because he's thinking _____ _____ to Brazil on his next vacation.

12. My cousin is a very good ice skater, but my brother and I _____. We just started _____ a few weeks ago. Before that, we _____ never _____ at all.

13. My mother doesn't know how to knit, but I _____. _____ been _____ little hats and sweaters all month because my cousin _____ _____ _____ _____ a baby.

J. SOUND IT OUT

Listen to each word and then say it.

full:	fool:
1. c<u>oo</u>k	1. s<u>oo</u>n
2. w<u>ou</u>ld	2. n<u>e</u>w
3. p<u>u</u>t	3. J<u>u</u>dy
4. f<u>oo</u>t	4. f<u>oo</u>d

Listen and put a circle around the word that has the same sound.

1. full:	p<u>oo</u>l	(cookies)	sh<u>oe</u>
2. fool:	t<u>oo</u>	c<u>ou</u>ld	bl<u>oo</u>d
3. good:	s<u>ou</u>p	sh<u>ou</u>ldn't	J<u>u</u>ne
4. hood:	fl<u>u</u>	s<u>ui</u>t	p<u>u</u>t
5. supermarket:	c<u>u</u>p	L<u>u</u>cy	<u>u</u>pstairs
6. w<u>o</u>man:	s<u>u</u>gar	tr<u>ue</u>	St<u>ua</u>rt

Now make a sentence using all the words you circled. Read the sentence aloud.

7. _____ _____ _____ _____ much _____ in the _____.

8. loose:	tw<u>o</u>	f<u>oo</u>t	b<u>u</u>s
9. would:	f<u>oo</u>d	b<u>oo</u>ks	sp<u>oo</u>ns
10. juice:	thr<u>ou</u>gh	sh<u>oo</u>k	m<u>u</u>st
11. neighborh<u>oo</u>d:	wh<u>o</u>	s<u>ou</u>venir	l<u>oo</u>ked
12. cool:	st<u>oo</u>d	aftern<u>oo</u>n	p<u>u</u>lse
13. took:	g<u>oo</u>d	t<u>oo</u>th	fr<u>ui</u>t
14. boot:	b<u>u</u>tter	c<u>ou</u>ldn't	S<u>u</u>san

Now make a sentence using all the words you circled. Read the sentence aloud.

15. _____ _____ _____ _____ _____ _____ this _____.

K. WHAT DOES IT MEAN?

Write the correct letter in the blank.

_j_	1. afford	a.	afraid
____	2. argue	b.	begin
____	3. consider	c.	do poorly
____	4. continue	d.	fight
____	5. discuss	e.	finish
____	6. exam	f.	fix
____	7. exhausted	g.	friendly and talkative
____	8. fail	h.	give back
____	9. frightened	i.	give lessons
____	10. hike	j.	have enough money
____	11. injure	k.	how much it costs
____	12. lately	l.	hurt
____	13. outgoing	m.	jog
____	14. prepared	n.	keep on
____	15. price	o.	meet
____	16. relax	p.	ready
____	17. repair	q.	recently
____	18. return	r.	rest
____	19. review	s.	someone who doesn't eat meat
____	20. run	t.	study again
____	21. run into	u.	take a long walk
____	22. stand in line	v.	talk about
____	23. start	w.	test
____	24. teach	x.	think about
____	25. use up	y.	very tired
____	26. vegetarian	z.	wait

CHECK-UP TEST: Chapters 9-10

A.   Complete the sentences.

Ex.   Don't worry about your mistakes. You can always cross _____them_____ _____out.____

I've had the flu for the past few days, but the doctor says I'll get ___over___ ____it____ soon.

1.   I always forget your address. Next time I'll write _____ _____.

2.   My daughter is waiting for me at the bus stop. I have to pick _____ _____ right away.

3.   Edward hasn't written in a long time. I hope we hear _____ _____ soon.

4.   I'll finish my homework in a little while, and then I'll hand _____ _____.

5.   Don't leave your clothes on the bed. You really should hang _____ _____.

6.   My teacher didn't like my composition. He says I have to do _____ _____.

7.   I don't see my aunt very often, but I ran _____ _____ yesterday at the bank.

8.   I want to wear this suit next weekend. Could you drop _____ _____ at the cleaner's?

9.   These problems are very difficult. I can't figure _____ _____.

10. Tom borrowed my skates last week, and he hasn't given _____ _____ to me yet.

11. I haven't talked to John in a long time. I'll call _____ _____ when I can get to a telephone.

B.   Complete the sentences.

┌─────────────────────────┐
│ /so/too/neither/either │
└─────────────────────────┘

Ex.   Mary just finished college, and _____so did_____ her boyfriend.

1.   I'm studying Algebra this semester, and _____ my friends.

2.   I won't be able to help you tomorrow, and _____ my wife.

3.   Jeffrey was very bored during science class, and his friends _____.

4.   Gloria can't stay very long, and her brother _____.

5.   I've been taking piano lessons for years, and _____ my brother and sister.

6.   Robert took a day off this week, and his wife _____.

7.   Ted has never failed an English exam, and _____ his sister.

8.   I want to go skiing this weekend, and _____ my neighbors.

9.   I'm not a very good dancer, and _____ my husband.

C. **Listen and complete the sentences.**

Ex. but his brother ___*doesn't.*___

1. but my friend _____.

2. but my parents _____.

3. but his sister _____.

4. but I _____.

5. but my mother _____.